D1555861

The Resilient Manager

THE RESILIENT MANAGER

Navigating the Challenges of Working Life

Adrian Furnham
Professor of Psychology,
University College London, UK

First published 2013 by
PALGRAVE MACMILLAN

Palgrave Macmillan in the UK is an imprint of Macmillan Publishers Limited, registered in England, company number 785998, of Houndmills, Basingstoke, Hampshire RG21 6XS.

Palgrave Macmillan in the US is a division of St Martin's Press LLC, 175 Fifth Avenue, New York, NY 10010.

Palgrave Macmillan is the global academic imprint of the above companies and has companies and representatives throughout the world.

Palgrave® and Macmillan® are registered trademarks in the United States, the United Kingdom, Europe and other countries.

ISBN 978–1–137–36106–6

This book is printed on paper suitable for recycling and made from fully managed and sustained forest sources. Logging, pulping and manufacturing processes are expected to conform to the environmental regulations of the country of origin.

A catalogue record for this book is available from the British Library.

A catalog record for this book is available from the Library of Congress.

Typeset by MPS Limited, Chennai, India.

For my mother Lorna Goodwin (1924–2011),
a woman of great resilience

Contents

Contents

Preface

This is the third of a trilogy. The first two were called *The Talented Manager* and *The Engaging Manager*. They follow the same format: a general 'essay', followed by 60–70 reflections on current business affairs. They have been categorized into six themes. What they have in common are my rather sceptical observation on current corporate life.

I speak at lots of conferences and do coaching and training work as well as other forms of consultancy. I also read the academic literature. And I work in a variety of institutions. All this gives me the material for my essays and reflections.

I must point out that I get enormous enjoyment out of writing them. First, I am less constrained by the academic fetishism of refereed journals, where to claim the sky is blue requires one to find an academic reference. Next, this form of writing means I can sail under the radar of the politically correct police, perhaps expressing a view that is '*verboten*' in the organization. Third, I never know quite what I believe about a topic until I am forced to write down my ideas in around 1000 words. Odd to not know what you believe until you start writing, but there it is: that is the way I do it.

As usual, I have many people to thank. But above all is Alison, who has read and vetted every essay. Some just passed the mark, some got a starred first, and alas, many did not make it. She is invaluable to me in all that I do. Eleanor Davey-Corrigan has put in a lot of effort to make this book more useful to managers, for which I am most grateful. And I am also grateful to my many students with whom I have discussed a number of these issues.

Adrian Furnham, London, 2013

Introduction

Stress at work is as inevitable as death and taxes. We all (occasionally) get stressed. Amen. But the interesting thing about it is: how often we get stressed, how significant (acute and chronic) that stress is, what the usual causes of that stress are and what, essentially, we can do (or do regularly) about it.

Stress affects the body, decisions and judgements, relationships and work performance. We now know a lot about the physiology of stress and how the hormones cortisol, noradrenaline and adrenaline impact on people over time. Stress is bad, so we need to know how to deal with it. Being stress resistant and able to cope with stress is good. That is at the heart of resilience. It is about coping and bouncing back after significant, as well as minor, setbacks. Resilience is a prophylactic against failure: a way of adapting and thriving, rather than ruminating or falling into depression.

Resilient people can self-regulate: they can control their impulses and emotions. And they tend to be optimistic. Employers want resilient staff. And most people want it too.

It has been argued that resilience has various components. It has to do (in part) with realistic *self confidence*, which is a realistic appraisal of achievements and choices. It is also about *self-esteem*, which is having a sense of one's purpose and contribution. Next, there is *self-efficacy*, which is the belief in one's own abilities and strengths. In addition, there is *self-control*, the belief that one is in control of one's life – captain of one's ship and master of one's fate.

Resilience is also about thinking straight. The power of Cognitive Behaviour Therapy (CBT) has shown how thinking errors or styles can have powerful positive and negative effects. These include frequently catastrophizing (i.e. getting things out of proportion), externalizing (i.e. blaming others for your own behaviours), generalizing to believe that small things always have large consequences, black-and-white thinking and so on.

A WORD ABOUT STOICISM

I have changed my mind about stoicism, a trait I once greatly admired. Stoics were followers of Zeno of Citium (300 BC) and believed in various clear virtues (or behaviour patterns?): imperturbability in the face of challenge, being (very) cool under fire, always making light of pain, having great fortitude, minimizing personal difficulties and concealing any form of anxiety, doubt and distress. To give a modern example, this means being more like older generations who tend not to complain so much, who do not demand immediate relief from low-level pain, and who refrain from clogging up doctors' surgeries with minor ailments and essentially psychological problems.

In the nineteenth century, heroes such as Captain Oates showed great stoicism derived from a public school ethos. This was about 'muscular Christianity' and the suppression of emotions, particularly any sign of vulnerability or weakness. It meant acceptance of casual, capricious, corporal punishment. Most of all, it was about the display of calm, control and disinterest in the face of danger – the stoic virtues/behaviour of showing imperturbability when challenged or threatened, always being cool under fire, minimizing difficulties, making light of any kind of pain, 'taking it like a man'.

Of course, this also means the concealment of anxiety, doubt and distress, tight control of emotional expression and never showing vulnerability – the British 'stiff upper lip' or the Aussie ideal of masculinity. But is that desirable and healthy at work, or even outside work for that matter? There is a psychological test that measures stoicism. Items include: 'It makes me uncomfortable when people express their emotions in front of me' and 'Expressing emotions is a sign of weakness.' Stoics disagree with the following statements: 'I believe that it is healthy to express one's emotions.' 'I like someone to hold me when I am upset.' 'I sometimes cry in public.' Other psychologists have distinguished between repressors and sensitizers when it comes to pain and problems.

The repression-sensitization dimension is a defence mechanism used in reducing anxiety. Repressors are stoics who respond to threat by blocking, denying, repressing and forgetting distressing events. They try to avoid the issues. Sensitizers, by contrast, respond by readily recognizing threat, having better recall of distressing events and 'letting it all hang out' – they approach, rather than avoid, situations.

Ian Hislop's *Stiff Upper Lip: The Emotional History of Britain* attempted to throw light on whether the British were ever stoics and, if indeed we were, whether we are now changing, turning into a lot of pathetic cry-babies – failures, people of low moral fibre with no stomach for the fight – or perhaps at last showing a healthy ability to cope with emotions?

Certainly one can see stoicism, or the lack of it, in the workplace. Some workers seem perpetually ill and constantly complaining while others are bonny and robust. Most managers want employees with a healthy mind in a healthy body – those who don't spend all their time weeping or consulting counsellors. Would it do us all good to go on a few 'stoics' coping skills' courses to learn this philosophy a little better?

The psychological literature seems rather negative about stoicism as a philosophy or, indeed, as a coping response. There are four reasons for thinking that it is a potentially maladaptive and undesirable way of dealing with the world:

1. Particularly for men, stoicism is associated with inertia in the face of medical symptoms. As has been noted, GP surgeries are full of women, yet A&E and Intensive Care are full of men. There are long-term costs to ignoring and downplaying symptoms ('only sissies go to doctors'). Men live on average six years less than women. There are various reasons for this, one of which includes the late detection of serious illness. Ignoring what your body is telling you is not sensible or virtuous.

2. The reluctance to talk about emotions may actually result from the inability to do so. High emotional intelligence is defined as being aware of one's own and others' emotions and also being able to manage one's own and others' emotions. Pretending that it is unwise, weak or unhealthy to talk about emotions may just be a bad cover for not knowing how to do it.

   It is well known that males are more likely to sit on the schizoid and autistic/Asperger's spectrum than females. Males may appear emotionally illiterate, unskilled and gauche. They may seem unable to recognize emotional signals in others or, even if they do, are unable to deal with them. And at work that is serious, which is why emotional intelligence is reckoned to be so important for managers.

   Men with a low emotional quotient (EQ) have manifold problems. Perhaps low EQ contributes to the higher number of men in prison, compared with women, and the higher rate for suicide and unemployment in males. There is all the difference in the world between *choosing* not to deal with emotions and being *unable* to do so.

3. Related to the above, emotional intelligence may be associated both with giving help to, and even seeking help from, colleagues at work. Management is a contact sport. We are all interdependent at work and need to give and receive support. Unwillingness to help others in distress surely does not help team spirit. It also means stoics will be avoided as they are more likely to be disparaging rather than helpful.

4. Stoical people can be seen as cold and arrogant. Many show off their toughness with displays of superiority. Their values of competition, control, dominance and power are particularly unattractive in today's workforce. Some even enjoy victimizing the odd, eccentric and weak who don't share their philosophy.

So, should we select stoics to join us in the workplace? Probably not!

BROKEN, MADE AND TESTED BY ADVERSITY

Business school, medical and military training share some interesting pedagogical characteristics, despite obvious and manifold differences between them. The drill sergeant may not appear to be very like the dental surgeon or the demographic strategist but may have a similar philosophy.

This is not about a love of case studies, be they military campaigns, bizarre patients or stories of failed companies. Nor does it involve dress codes or social rituals. It is that students are put under pressure. The pressure is in part an attempt to simulate real-life situations: too much to do with too few people in too much time, being sleep deprived and being asked to make decisions with serious consequences.

This is certainly not how non-vocational students experience education. What pressures are put on the art historian or the classicist? (True, some language students may experience some difficulty if parachuted into a foreign city and told to get on with it.)

The reason for putting students under pressure is essentially twofold:

1. To test their aptitude for the career they have chosen. If you can't stand the heat, get out of the kitchen. This is what it is going to be like and if you don't like it, quit now. This is the dry run, the dress rehearsal. It will all be like this or more so. Are you sure it is for you?
2. To improve their coping skills – to teach them how to react to pressure. There is more talk of the concept of resilience at work. Perhaps it is a backlash against the 'stress at work' bleating from the stress industry.

So what is resilience? It's about adapting to coping and learning from adversity. It is about 'bouncing back' and 'continuing forward'. Keep calm and carry on.

Some years ago a synonymous concept was popular. It was called '*hardiness*'. Hardy people believe they have personal control over their lives. They are instrumentalists, not fatalists. They have a sense of coherence, and an ability to manage their own and others' emotions. This ability to regulate means they can easily forge, sustain and count on relationships with others. Also they can cope with change. They use the word (and mean it) 'challenging', not 'threat'.

Resilient people are comfortable in their own skin. They are neither arrogant nor self-doubting and they feel competent, even optimistic, that they can get through stuff. They can cope with ambiguity, get help when they need it and make good decisions.

The question, of course, is whether resilience can be taught. Studies of resilience show that the toughest and most adaptive people have known testing times, often in childhood. An unstable family life, caused by poverty, war or difficult relationships, tests a young person. Death, divorce and downward mobility all bring out the best and worst in a child. These things can break the sensitive, vulnerable youth or forge the stable one. If you have been through the darkest night when you are at your most vulnerable, little can scare you after that.

Resilience is about head and heart. It is about being in touch with your emotions and being able to talk about them. It is about detecting the emotional signals in yourself and others *and* knowing what to do about them.

Resilience is not about denial, being tough or repressing emotions. And it is not about a 'big boys don't cry' macho boastfulness. There is a dark side of stoicism which is sometimes confused with resilience. Stoicism is more about emotional non-involvement and control, lack of emotional expressivity, fortitude and emotional concealment.

Resilience, on the other hand, is about understanding and harnessing emotions. It's what is taught these days in the ubiquitous and very popular CBT. It's about reassessing how you think about people.

Both school and university are places that usually test a person's ability to deal with adversity. Bullying, failure and rejection are the lot of almost all students. And learning how to cope, even thrive, is really part of the syllabus . . . the playing fields of Eton and all that.

So what is there left to teach the postgraduate? Is it all too late? Emotionally literate and stable people are already formed. So what is still to be learnt? First, there is the complex nature of organizational life. Most institutions have ways of dealing with people in difficulty. The trick is to find out how, when or where to gain access. Second, the people you go through training with (boot camp) are likely to remain a crucial source of social support for years. After all, you know all about them and they know all about you. You have faced the bleak odds together and, one hopes, survived. Third, it is about knowing your tipping point . . . and that of others.

THE DEVELOPMENT OF RESILIENCE

There are a number of recent books on this topic. Indeed, it has attracted so much academic attention that there is now a 540-page *Handbook of Adult Resilience* edited by Reich, Zautra & Hall (2010) containing 24 chapters. They are concerned with issues such as whether resilience is a personality trait, a cognitive process or a learnt skill? Is it a process that causes positive adaptation or is it an outcome of experience?

There are also many more simple popular books. Thus, Neenan (2009) defines resilience as a set of flexible cognitive, behavioural and emotional responses to acute or chronic adversities, which can be unusual or commonplace. Essentially, it is about the attitude you adopt to cope with adversity. He argues that resilience is not a special gift but a capacity that can be learnt by anyone. It should be seen as coming back, rather than bouncing back, from adversity. And it is not just about dealing with adversity; it is about seeking new experiences and opportunities in order to learn and grow. It is about how to interpret everyday events. To a large extent it is about managing negative emotions and being able to distinguish what is and what is not in one's control. It is about learning from past experiences.

He ends with 10 simple but useful summary statements:

1. Resilience is a capacity that everybody can learn.
2. Resilience is coming back, rather than bouncing back, from adversity.
3. It is not just about dealing with adversity, but about seeking opportunities/experiences and taking risks.
4. Attitudes, beliefs and the way you look at the world are at the heart of resilience.
5. It is not only about attitudes but about behaviour: acting in support of your resilient attitudes.
6. Resilience is about managing negative emotions.
7. It is important to distinguish what is within and outside your personal control.
8. All experiences are useful – learn from setbacks and victories.
9. Develop 'can do' self-beliefs about achieving stretching goals and targets.
10. Maintain your resilient outlook, whatever comes your way.

Others have very much the same ideas. Clarke & Nicholson (2010) have a 10-point plan to increase resilience.

1. Visualize success, thinking about whom you benchmark yourself against, how you view your own capabilities and performance, and the way you come across to others.
2. Boost your self-esteem by listing things you are good at and recognizing what others appreciate and value about you.
3. Enhance your self-efficacy by taking control of your life. It is suggested that you need to get rid of six 'drag anchors':
   (a) I am the victim of my personal history.
   (b) There's so much to do, it's not even worth trying.
   (c) I get only one shot at this.
   (d) There's a right answer to everything.

(e) I am on my own.

(f) This isn't fair.

4. Become more optimistic because resilience is the ability to reframe things, most notably moving from feelings of disappointment to seeing opportunities.

5. Manage stress by reducing stress-inducing things, such as displaying hostility to others, being too much of a perfectionist, being unable to listen to others, having a tendency to hide your feelings and having difficulty in relaxing.

6. Improve your decision-making by trying honest risk assessment and asking others for help. It also helps to work on being more rational and more intuitive.

7. Ask for help and reach out to others in your network.

8. Deal with conflict assertively and flexibly using collaborative conflict (that is healthy disagreement).

9. Take up life-long learning. Invest time and resources in it.

10. Be yourself – be authentic.

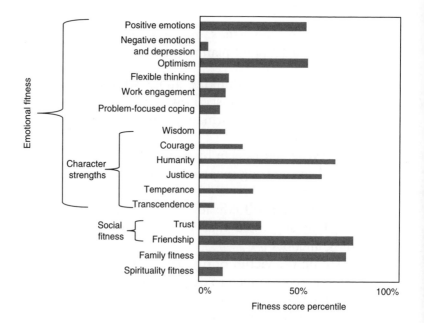

Martin Seligman (2011), the founder of positive psychology, is very interested in this area. In his latest book, *Flourish*, he describes how one might assess a person's fitness score (p. 138).

He stresses the importance of emotional and social fitness, both of which can be assessed by means of some simple questionnaires.

So, to assess emotional fitness Seligman invites the reader to:

Rate the statements in the following table in terms of how you usually think.

1 = Not like me at all. **2** = A little like me. **3** = Somewhat like me. **4** = Mostly like me. **5** = Very much like me.

Item	Scale				
When bad things happen to me, I expect more bad things to happen	1	2	3	4	5
I have no control over the things that happen to me	1	2	3	4	5
I respond to stress by making things worse than they are	1	2	3	4	5
In uncertain times, I usually expect the best	1	2	3	4	5
If something can go wrong for me, it will	1	2	3	4	5
I rarely count on good things happening to me	1	2	3	4	5
Overall, I expect more good things to happen to me than bad	1	2	3	4	5
My work is one of the most important things in my life	1	2	3	4	5
I would choose my current work again if I had the chance	1	2	3	4	5
I am committed to my job	1	2	3	4	5
How I do in my job influences how I feel	1	2	3	4	5
I was obsessed with a certain idea or project for a short time but later lost interest	1	2	3	4	5
It is difficult for me to adjust to changes	1	2	3	4	5
I usually keep my feelings to myself	1	2	3	4	5

To assess social emotional fitness, Seligman invites the reader to:

Please indicate how strongly you agree or disagree with each of the following statements.

Item	Scale				
My work makes the world a better place	1	2	3	4	5
I trust my fellow colleagues to look out for my welfare and safety	1	2	3	4	5
My closest friends are people in my unit/ department	1	2	3	4	5
Overall, I trust my immediate superior	1	2	3	4	5
My life has a lasting meaning	1	2	3	4	5
I believe that in some way my life is closely connected to all humanity and the whole world	1	2	3	4	5
The job I am doing has lasting meaning	1	2	3	4	5
I am very close to my family	1	2	3	4	5
I am confident that the army will take care of my family	1	2	3	4	5
The organization puts too much of a burden on my family	1	2	3	4	5
The organization makes it easy for my family to do well	1	2	3	4	5

Note: This questionnaire was designed for use in the American military but can be easily adapted for use with other groups.

The idea of *Flourish* is to maximize well-being and minimize misery. It is about becoming a rugged individual who does not scare easily. Seligman places a lot of emphasis on identifying strengths in yourself and others. Other techniques such as counting your blessings daily, making a gratitude visit and writing a forgiveness letter are well known to positive psychologists. Again, the message is that resilience can be learned.

BECOMING A TALENTED LEADER

There are many ways to develop staff with the potential to be resilient. Already proven, talented leaders provide much the same story and explanation of the factors that influenced them. Studies across organizations in different sectors and across different corporate and national cultures – even different epochs – reveal the same story. Talented leaders mention six powerful learning experiences:

1. *Early work experience.* This may be a 'part-time' job while at school, a relatively unskilled summer holiday job while at university, or one of the first jobs they ever had. For some it was the unadulterated tedium or monotony that powerfully motivated them to avoid similar jobs in the future. For others it was a particular work style or process that they have retained all their lives. This is something that can be identified and selected.

2. *The experience of other people.* This is nearly always an immediate boss, but can also be a colleague or peer. These people are almost always remembered as either *very bad* or *very good* – both teach lessons. The moral of this from a development perspective is to find a series of excellent role-model, mentor-type bosses for the talent group.

3. *Short-term assignments.* These include project work, standing in for another or interim management. This experience takes people out of their comfort zone and exposes them to issues and problems they have never confronted, so they learn quickly. For some it is the lucky break – serendipity provides an opportunity to find a new skill or passion.

4. *First major line assignment.* This is often the first promotion, foreign posting or departmental move to a higher position. It is frequently cited because suddenly the stakes were higher, everything was more complex, novel and ambiguous. There were more pressures and the person was ultimately accountable. Suddenly, the difficulties of management became real. The idea, then, is to think through appropriate

'stretch assignments' for talented people as soon as they arrive.

5. *Hardships of various kinds.* This is about attempting to cope in a crisis, which may be professional or personal. It teaches the real value of things: technology, loyal staff, supportive head offices. The experiences are those of battle-hardened soldiers or the 'been there, done that' brigade. Hardship teaches many lessons: how resourceful and robust some people can be and how others panic and cave in. It teaches some people to admire a fit and happy organization when they see it. It teaches them to distinguish between needs and wants. It teaches about stress management and the virtues of stoicism, hardiness and a tough mental attitude.

6. *Management development.* Some leaders remember and quote their MBA experience; far fewer cite some specific (albeit expensive) course. One or two quote the experience of receiving 360-degree feedback. More recall a coach, because they were either so good or so awful. This is bad news for poor trainers, business school teachers and coaches.

7. To the extent that leadership is acquired, developed and learnt – rather than 'gifted' – it is achieved mainly through work experiences. Inevitably, some experiences are better than others because they teach different lessons in different ways. Some people seem to acquire these valuable experiences despite, rather than as a result of, company policy.

8. Experiential learning takes time, but timing is important. It is not a steady, planned accumulation of insights and skills, and some experiences teach little or, indeed, bad habits.

Three factors conspire to defeat the experiential model: First, both young managers and their bosses want to short-circuit experience: learn faster, cheaper, better – hence the appeal of the one-minute manager, the one-day MBA and the short course. Second, many human resources (HR) professionals see this approach as disempowering them because they like to be 'in charge' of the leadership development programme. Third, some see experience as a test, not a developmental exercise.

A critical component of potential is the *ability to learn from experience*. Equally, every move, promotion or challenge should be assessed by the learning potential. The capacity to meet and learn from a challenge is more important to potential than past experience at an identical task.

COPING

Whether people suffer from stress or not is largely dependent on their coping strategies. Therefore, psychologists have spent considerable effort in describing and categorizing different strategies, some of which are thought to be 'successful' and adaptive, and others not. These strategies are stress-specific concepts; hence they tend to be better predictors of occupational stress than broadband stress concepts.

One distinction is between *problem-focused* coping (aimed at problem-solving or doing something to alter the source of stress) and *emotion-focused* coping (aimed at reducing or managing the emotional distress that is associated with, or cued by, a particular situation). Others have pointed out that this distinction is too simple. Thus, Carver, Scherer & Weintraub (1989) have distinguished between both types of coping: some emotion-focused responses involve denial, others involve positive reinterpretation of events, and still others involve the seeking out of social support. Similarly, problem-focused coping can potentially involve several distinct activities, such as planning, taking direct action, seeking assistance, screening out particular activities, and sometimes stopping acting for an extended period. The 15 strategies outlined by Carver *et al.* (1989) detail both adaptive and non-adaptive coping strategies:

1. Positive reinterpretation and growth.
2. Active coping.
3. Planning.
4. Seeking social support for emotional problems.
5. Seeking social support for instrumental problems.
6. Suppression of competing activities.
7. Religion.
8. Acceptance.
9. Mental disengagement.
10. Focus on/venting emotion.
11. Behavioural disengagement.
12. Denial.
13. Restraint coping.
14. Alcohol use.
15. Humour.

It is argued that, for various reasons, individuals tend to adopt, and habitually use, a few of these coping patterns, which may or may not be successful. However, it does seem that people can be taught or trained to relinquish less successful coping strategies and adopt others. Resilience and coping are clearly related: the resilient person has more and better coping strategies than the less resilient person.

OPTIMISM: A BUFFER AGAINST STRESS

One personal factor that seems to play an important role in determining resistance to stress is the familiar dimension of *optimism/pessimism*. Optimists are hopeful in their outlook on life, interpret a wide range of situations in a positive light, and tend to expect favourable outcomes and results. Pessimists, by contrast, interpret many situations negatively, and expect unfavourable outcomes and results. Recent studies indicate that optimists are much more stress resistant than pessimists. For example, optimists are much less likely than pessimists to report physical illness and symptoms during highly stressful periods, such as final exams. Optimists and pessimists seem to adopt sharply contrasting tactics for coping with stress. Optimists concentrate on *problem-focused coping* – making and enacting specific plans for dealing with sources of stress. In addition, they seek *social support* – the advice and help of friends and others – and refrain from engaging in other activities until current problems are solved and stress is reduced. Pessimists tend to adopt rather different strategies, such as giving up in their efforts to reach goals with which stress is interfering, and denying that the stressful events have even occurred. Further, they have different attributional styles: the optimist attributes success internally and failure externally, and vice versa. Indeed, that is how optimism and pessimism are both measured and maintained.

HARDINESS: VIEWING STRESS AS CHALLENGE

Another individual difference factor that seems to distinguish stress-resistant people from those who are more susceptible to its harmful effects is known as '*hardiness*' (Kobasa 1979). This term refers to a cluster of characteristics rather than just one. Hardy people seem to differ from others in three respects. They show higher levels of *commitment* – deeper involvement in their jobs and other life activities; *control* – the belief that they can, in fact, influence important events in their lives and the outcomes they experience; and *challenge* – they perceive change as a challenge and an opportunity to grow rather than as a threat to their security.

Together, these characteristics tend to arm hardy people with high resistance to stress. People classified as high in hardiness report better health than those low in hardiness, even when they encounter major stressful life changes. Hardiness is a useful concept for understanding the impact of stress. However, recent evidence suggests that commitment and a sense of control are the most important components of hardiness. Thus, further research concerned with this personal dimension and its role in resistance to stress should focus primarily on these aspects.

There may well be other individual differences which are highly predictive of stress, but the ones mentioned above have attracted most research attention. Further, these different dimensions are, no doubt, intercorrelated.

THE CONSEQUENCES OF STRESS

The consequences of work stress are felt by individuals, their families, the organizations they work for, and the economy as a whole. Indeed, it is even possible through absenteeism and performance-related measures to calculate the effects of stress. It runs into many hundreds of billions of dollars, pounds and marks.

For the individual, the effects of work stress classically occur in many areas, although there may be strong individual differences. Attempts to 'manage' (control and reduce) stress essentially happen at two levels. First, some organizations focus on individual employees, trying to help them learn better techniques to prevent or reduce their personal stress levels. Second, others focus on the job or the organization as a whole in attempting to reduce stress.

The most commonly used techniques include the following.

Lifestyle (diet and exercise) changes: A healthy mind (psyche) is found in a healthy body. Hence, organizations attempt to help people with better living. This includes a better diet (less salt, fat, sugar) and the reduction or elimination of alcohol, tobacco and other 'recreational' drugs. They do this via their canteen arrangements as well as through legislation (no-smoking buildings). Others install expensive fitness centres with regular programmes for employees. Certainly, there are enough research findings that demonstrate the fact that physically fit people suffer less physical stress from physical stressors, although the relationship and the explanation between psychological stressors, fitness and stress is less clear.

Relaxation and meditation: Potentially stressed workers are taught how to meditate and relax. The former involves clearing one's head of external thoughts and concentrating on inner stillness. Relaxation techniques can be physical, involving such things as stretching, deep breathing and even laughing. People tend to choose techniques they feel are most suitable for them, although indeed they may not be.

Cognitive self-therapy: Sports psychologists as well as clinicians have shown how effective certain cognitive or thinking strategies are. Most place emphasis on how the way we conceive a stressor can be very maladaptive but can be changed. Thus, people are often asked to describe stressors and to think about them in different terms. Thus, 'stressful' becomes 'challenging', 'impossible' becomes 'possible'. Often, emphasis is placed on making people feel that stressors are temporary and controllable, not stable and eternal. People who have tendencies towards perfectionism often need this type of therapy.

Behaviour therapy: This approach attempts to overcome stress by focusing on behaviours that reduce it. Just as people who are socially phobic or have panic attacks can be taught ways to overcome that very specific type of stress, so all people can be taught 'little tricks' that help them overcome the stress. Certainly, one focus is on out-of-work activities such as leisure and vacations. The impact of the personal life on the working life should not be underestimated.

TOUGHEN UP, LIGHTEN UP, AND BUCK UP

The ability to survive and thrive at work is fundamental. Resilient people are happier, healthier and more productive. Organizations wisely strive to select resilient people and also help to increase that resilience. It is partly a skill, an attitude and a personality trait. Some people are clearly better than others at learning to become resilient and staying that way.

REFERENCES

Carver, C., Scherer, M. & Weintraub, J. (1989) Assessing coping strategies. *Journal of Personality and Social Psychology*, 56, 267–283.

Clarke, J. & Nicholson, J. (2010) *Resilience: Bounce Back from Whatever Life Throws at You*. London: Crimson.

Kobasa, S. (1979) Stressful life events, personality and health: An enquiry into hardiness. *Journal of Personality and Social Psychology*, 37, 114–128.

Neenan, M. (2009) *Developing Resilience*. London: Routledge.

Reich, J., Zautra, A. & Hall, J. (Eds) (2010) *Handbook of Adult Resilience*. London: Guilford.

Seligman, M. (2011) *Flourish*. London: Nicholas Brealey.

PART I

Building a Team

People can be both the greatest source of strength and support but also the greatest source of stress at work. It all sounds rather easy: all you need to do is attract, select, engage and motivate a group into a high-performing team that is superior to your competitors! It starts with selecting the right people. Easier said than done – the divorce statistics speak volumes on that score. People are complex. They are on their best behaviour at the interview.

The resilient manager needs to select people like him/ herself: able to ride the waves, stay focused and upbeat, and reframe setbacks as opportunities to learn. Spend time on recruitment and selection – it is worth it.

A. A GOOD LUNCH

Theatre directors faced with putting on a great classic often go a trifle 'off-piste' in an attempt to bring something new to the play. So they set *Macbeth* in a Disneyland theme park or try *Anthony and Cleopatra* in the nude.

Management consultants, too, often feel the urge to add a bit of novelty and excitement to the recruitment and selection business. Every so often they think of daft activities to provide 'new and rich insight' into candidates' 'real abilities, personality and motives'. This goes well beyond asking some rather bizarre questions and may involve a rather odd task, perhaps with others, in a quasi-assessment-centre situation.

Selection is an area full of superstition, bogus claims and sheer piffle. We all know that choosing people is difficult. We all know that the heart can rule the head. We know that people are complex and capricious . . . and that they are hardly at their most natural and sincere during a selection interview.

In the old days, however, when one 'good chap' could spot another, all you required was a good lunch to assess what is now called variously 'corporate culture fit', 'high potential', or 'executive talent'. What you wanted to know was: do you trust this fella, are you on the same page with regard to ethics and values and is he (always a he) one of your people?

It was not, as has been supposed, a close-up inspection of the candidates' cufflinks and tie to see whether he had been to a 'college on the right side of "The High"' or was a member of a 'good club'. Nor was it about knowledge of the wine list or pushing peas onto the fork. That most elemental of social activities, sharing hot food together, offers opportunities to assess potentially important skills.

Social skills, emotional intelligence and charm . . . can the candidate do small talk? Never ignore or downplay the ability to do chit-chat, to pick up on cues and keep a conversation going, to understand the importance of turn-taking, to express an interest in others and be interesting, to be aware of their own and others' emotions and motives.

One organization includes a test based on chit-chat in its selection process. In pairs, people are asked to pick a card on which there is a question. The questions are pretty simple: What characteristics did you inherit from your father? Have you ever been seriously ill? What is your greatest life achievement? Each person has a very different question. The task is threefold: (1) to get the answer to your question while (2) disguising so that the other person has no idea what it is and (3) listening to find out what their question is. It is a game of listening for hidden agendas during bland, everyday conversations. It is a very important life and business skill.

Next, a one- to two-hour lunch offers people the opportunity to visit many issues that may seem inappropriate in a traditional, stilted office atmosphere. For example, a chat about previous jobs, bosses they admired, policies they thought innovative, what factors had the most influence over their career and, indeed, their out-of-work activities. Also, people drop their guard in such events, unable to keep up various pretences for all that time.

It may also show their understanding of etiquette and politeness. Most would (usually) refuse alcohol, but what if the host said: 'I fancy a glass of wine, will you join me?' The skilled executive knows the power of mirroring when it comes to negotiation and general 'friend raising'.

Dealing with staff . . . it is possible over the course of lunch that the candidate might interact with a range of serving staff. Does the candidate treat them like 'plebs' or is the candidate intimidated by them? Is the candidate annoyed by over- or under- attentiveness? What does the candidate think of how the restaurant is run? How does the candidate react to tipping?

Peculiarities will out at luncheon. It is difficult to believe that food fetishes are not related to social difficulties after watching an episode of the Channel 4 television series *Come Dine with Me*. Strong dislikes, intolerances and restrictions may reveal rigidities of one sort or another.

It is quite possible to bring up issues of health over a meal, as well as other habits. This is important stuff, especially if the job involves a lot of travel to foreign countries, entertainment and selling.

Is the cost of time and money worth it? And what about the retributive, litigious interviewee who, having been rejected, is convinced it was pure prejudice against teetotal vegans who insist on bringing their own cutlery to meals?

And do not forget that an interview, be it over lunch or not, gives the candidates a much better understanding of the interviewers who may turn out to be their boss. Both parties may disclose more, which must help good decision-making. Unfortunately, however, interviewers themselves often appear too guarded and socially insecure to carry off luncheon interviews successfully.

So does the old-fashioned lunch allow a recruiter to get a much better idea of the social and negotiation skills of a (reasonably) senior manager? Of course it does. A good investment? For a major job, certainly.

B. INTERVIEW LIES

How much deception in selection is there? How many porky pies are told by whom? There are certainly enough nouns to choose from when thinking about the act of deceit in the job interview (or elsewhere). There are the 'grown-up' words for the articulate and literate nit-picker, such as 'casuistry', 'perfidy' or 'sophistry' . . . or perhaps the detached, academic kind of words, such as 'dissimulation', 'falsehood' and 'understatement' . . . or you may prefer something a little richer, such as 'whopper', 'humbug' or 'scam'.

We all recall memorable phrases people used when caught out – like Churchill's 'terminological inexactitude' or Sir Robert Armstrong being 'economical with the truth'.

Most lies in interviews are high-stake lies. The nature and function of the lie, of course, depends on the type and purpose of the interview. The interview with the policeman is different from that of the journalist. Being interviewed by a potential employer or a tax authority can tempt people to 'adjust the truth' for many reasons.

High stakes means taking a serious calculation about potential important gains and losses. In some interviews it's a game. Politicians are masters of the art. They believe they have to be.

We know quite a lot about the characteristics of successful liars. Certainly, the best are natural performers with acting ability. They can convey just the right and timely emotional expression. And they do not have 'stage-fright' at being confronted with 'issues' in interviews. Often they are good-looking because attractive people are judged (unfairly, certainly) to be more honest. Naturally, they are highly confident and fluent. Many, being competitive, really enjoy the thrill of the interview and being able to 'dupe' the less successful interviewer. They intuitively know how to appear trustworthy.

Max Eggert, an expert on selection, has argued that there are many different types of lies. They make a good checklist for the potential interviewer.

1. *White lies.* These are found in the 'puff' statement that gormless people are encouraged to write on their CV: 'I am a totally committed team player.' 'I have excellent social skills and the ability to read people.' 'I am utterly trustworthy and loyal.' The question, of course, is: 'Who says and where is the evidence?' The best solution is to ignore all this flim-flam and say: 'I will be the judge of that, thank you.'
2. *Altruistic lies.* These are lies that attempt a cover-up, but look as if they are helping others. So rather than saying they left their last job because their manager was a bully, or the company was patently dodgy, the candidate says that they resigned to look for new challenges.
3. *Lies of omission.* For many people, these are the most frequent and easiest of lies. They might omit details of school or university grades because they had poor marks. Whole periods of their life are obfuscated. The most common lie concerns dates, often to disguise the fact that the candidate seemed to spend a surprisingly short amount of time in a succession of jobs. It is no more and no less than concealment.

4. *Defensive lies.* The defensive lie is one that conceals through generalizations or vagaries. Ask a person about their previous boss's management style, their reason for leaving or their health record, and you are often faced with a string of vague expressions, such as 'like others in the company' or 'much the same as my co-workers' or 'at that time'. Ask vague questions and you'll get defensive lies.

5. *Impersonation lies.* This is also called 'the transfer lie' and occurs mostly where people take credit for others' work. For example, statements such as 'I doubled sales over the year' or 'I was responsible for a budget of over three million.' All others in the hierarchy are forgotten in these lies. And it is often difficult to establish the facts as to who exactly was responsible for particular successes (and disasters, which are – of course – omitted).

6. *Embedded lies.* This is a clever subterfuge to confuse the interviewer. So, 'I really enjoyed my time in Oxford' could refer to a first job in the 'city of dreaming spires' where s/he was a mere underling. The idea is to suggest than an experience, qualification or achievement was very different from the actuality. 'It was good fun being with the BBC' could mean practically anything from 'I once went to a show there' to 'they filmed at my school.'

7. *Errors of commission or fact.* This is rather childish lying. These are explicit, verifiably false claims. For example, about qualifications you don't have, about starting up or working for companies that never existed, about skills that don't exist. They are the most blatant form of lie.

8. *Definition lies.* This is the sport of lawyers and of presidents. What precisely does it mean 'to have sex' with someone? What is 'a company turnaround'? What does it mean to be 'in the latest group'? This approach involves working with a very specific and

obscure definition so that for all intents and purposes you are telling the truth.

9. *Proxy lies.* This is where the candidates get others to lie for them. Referees are usually previous employers but they could be former teachers. Candidates may skilfully work on their referees' poor memory, vanity or other bribes to persuade them to obfuscate.

So give up 'bullshit bingo'. Have your 'porkies card' available at your next interview. Try to work out the particular 'impression management' preferences of every candidate in this cat-and-mouse game called 'the interview'.

C. JOB HISTORY

You are interviewing someone for a senior position. Three candidates are on the shortlist. They are all intelligent, experienced, qualified and personable. They have been through a reasonably rigorous process: due diligence, multiple interviews, evidence-based competency analysis. It has cost a 'pretty penny', but you believe it is worth it to get the right person. The cost of a failure is too high for all concerned.

However, they have rather different work histories. Candidate A has really only had two jobs in his 20-year working life, 18 of those latter years in the same job. By contrast, candidate B has worked for eight different organizations over that period, staying two to three years in each. Candidate C is the intermediate: working in four organizations for roughly five years each.

On further inspection you notice that not only were the organizations different for B and C but so were the job functions. So you have evidence of 'chopping and changing' in candidate B vs 'steady as you go' in candidate C. Does this mean that C has happily left the comfort of his or her silo and has an all-round perspective of how big, complex organizations work?

What do you conclude: is this multiple job-holding an index of risk taking vs risk aversion? Or is it a turn-your-hand-to-anything generalist vs a narrow specialist? Does frequent job change measure ambition? Or does it reveal the inability to stick at anything? The question, of course, is why did they change and, more importantly, whose decision was it?

Some job candidates will tell you it's important to stick at a job in an organization for at least two years, otherwise it looks bad on the CV; Some say three years; others, five. But why? Does it indicate that they didn't like it or didn't fit in? Or that they couldn't really make a difference in that period? Or worse, that they were 'found out'?

What if you stay in the same job, the same department and the same organization for 10 years? Is it better, or more unusual, to be promoted from within or is it an organizational policy to get senior people from outside? Maybe this all depends on the job and the sector, and, indeed, the state of the economy. In some sectors the only way you climb the greasy pole is by jumping ship regularly. And in flat organizations you are expected to stay for longer periods in the same job as there are fewer rungs on the ladder.

The answer to many of these questions lies in *why* people stay or leave. To be eminently employable means you have to *get* a job and then *retain* it. Many know the power and safety net of the probationary period, which gives both parties a second chance.

The question is: Does getting a job involve different skills and attributes than retaining one? How do you get a job in the first place? Easy: ability, education, experience. You are lured for your skills and also for your outlook. But how do you beat others at the job interview? How do you get to be *the* chosen one?

The answer is usually enhanced presentational skills. Yes, past job performance is important, as are references.

Yes, you need to pass any assessment centre types of test – you need to be stable, bright, and conscientious . . . or appear to be so. But you are also going to need charm, self-confidence and social intelligence.

You need to portray all aspects of social desirability, that is, show you are likeable, honest and caring. You should buy one of those books on 'brilliant answers to tough interview questions'. And you will need to know something about impression management. You also need to look good. Cue the body language component of the management course . . . and the right outfit and accessories.

So who gets picked in the end: Good-looking shysters? Silver-tongued psychopaths? Over-rehearsed, pathologically ambitious actors? Sometimes. It's a political game. Self-assured people with the gift of the gab are snapped up. The hesitant, self-doubting, albeit talented introverts get left behind. They may have better references, more qualifications, higher scores on the assessment centre exercises, but they just don't *come across* well . . . and that really matters.

But getting a job is not the same as keeping it. It is not the same as getting a promotion from within. Good-looking, charming Machiavellians may have the advantage at interview but they do get found out. They make bad decisions. It is all about them, not others. They can be disruptive and inclined to dispute if met with resistance, and they can be breathtakingly insensitive, selfish and manipulative – bastards, bullies and belittlers.

People keep jobs if they are conscientious, socially rewarding and fit in. The Machiavellian, the psychopath and the narcissist are not like this at all. But they can appear immensely charming. They know how to stand out at an interview. They know the lines well. But they don't follow through.

The answer lies in why people say they 'move on' from one job to another. Between the deeply evasive interviewee when asked specific and difficult questions. Invest in a spot of serious checking with previous employers. You may soon see a yawning incongruity between the CV and interview, and the report of others.

D. PERSONALITY OF REFERENCE WRITERS

The personal reference: Is it an invaluable, disinterested source of extremely useful information on potential candidates about a person's *real* personality, ability, values and work style? Or is it a pointless paper chase that legal requirements have rendered worse than useless?

From the teacher's input on the university application form to the 'good character' statement in certain court appearances, the reference remains a cornerstone in the whole selection and appraisal process. It should be an ideal tool that you can obtain cheaply and easily (nowadays mainly by phone) – the reports of (many) others who (really) know the person in a variety of circumstances. Those who have studied, worked and played with the candidate . . . seen them in different moods, in different situations, facing different obstacles.

If the best predictor of future behaviour is past behaviour, surely detailed reports on that past behaviour will provide the very best prognostic information that a selector could possibly want.

Ask anybody 'Who knows you best?' and men say, 'My wife', though interestingly not all women say, 'My husband'. Aah, but would they (ever) give a frank appraisal of their husbands, except, of course, in the divorce court?

One of the problems with referees is essentially the same as with interviewers. It is the impact of the personality of the referee on the reference. How insightful, honest and literate is the referee? Not all referees are equally perceptive about people. Nerdy, tetchy types can find (all) people problematic. They may have little insight into others' emotions and motivations; hence their references would be worthless.

Referees can have a very different 'take' on the same person, even when given very much the same data. Some have a shrewd, clinical assessment, soon getting below the surface acting. Others seem impervious to the beliefs, values and motives of people they work with and for.

Next, there is the problem of literacy. References are written or spoken. But no matter how insightful a person, if they have a restricted, limited or amateur vocabulary, they may never really be able to communicate their impressions.

Also, their mood – indeed, their moodiness – can have an effect. Get them on the wrong day and their 'negative affectivity' is projected onto others. Find them after a morale-boosting success and this positivity spills over into the candidate reference.

References are meant to describe behaviours, but of course they can be just as much an index of liking and 'fit'. By-and-large we are attracted to people like us. Extroverts seek out fun-loving, optimistic party-goers. The tender-minded, empathic, agreeable types search for like-minded companions.

So the personality of the referee has a powerful impact on the style, tone and, indeed, encoded messages in the reference. For easy proof, compare half a dozen references for the same person and note the differences.

There is another problem which has evolved from our old friend sociobiology again: *mating interest*. Would it surprise you to find that men (of all ages) write longer and more positive references about younger (prettier) women than all other types? Yet another problem is *tit-for-tat reciprocity*: I do you a good turn (i.e. write a spuriously positive reference) and at a later date I expect you to return the favour.

Of course this happens. Observe some secret societies or try looking at authors' reviews of each other's books (the comments on the back cover). I scratch your back, you comb mine.

Some researchers have even proposed that a good way to assess people's suitability for managerial positions may be to content analyze their letters of reference. See what they say and how they say it. The results may give real insight into their personality and their values.

But could you make references any more reliable? One way is to promise anonymity, but this remains ever more difficult to guarantee, given the porous nature of email. Another is for referees to rank people, or say whether they are in the top 1 per cent, 5 per cent, 10 per cent or 25 per cent of candidates they have ever known. The trouble with this is that everyone is 'above average' and grade inflation has crept in.

Better still, give referees a forced choice, especially for negative behaviours. Is the individual more likely to (a) take excessive 'sickies' or (b) liberate office stationery? More likely to (a) turn in shoddy work or (b) bad mouth the boss? Overall, this method can generate some really interesting stuff, but there are some ethical and statistical problems associated with it.

Some recommend classifying the content of referees by counting the words. For example, a number of references to time issues may indicate a problem. Some referees – particularly the English – have learnt to code negative features brilliantly. 'Always gets there in the end' could mean 'dim-witted plodder', or 'slap-dash impulsive'.

The idea of the double-meaning quip is to signal to others the real issue. So references become a code of the kind you find in newspaper obituaries: 'He loved life' means he was a disinhibited, amoral hedonist; 'He never married' means he was gay; 'He was a *bon viveur*' means he was a drunk.

So, like every aspect of selection, obtaining a simple, accurate reference is not necessarily straightforward. Some simple points: First, begin by deciding what precisely you want to know about a candidate. Second, find the people who might have that information and do a bit of homework on them. Ask them clearly what you want to know in different ways. Listen carefully to what they are saying. And bear in mind you may end up knowing more about the referees than the candidates!

E. POOR SELECTION

There are three major problems (discussed below) associated with the traditional selection method ordained by HR that can often lead to the hiring of potentially 'derailing' leaders. People can be selected who appear to fit all the hiring criteria, but who hold the potential to 'derail' after they join the organization. The errors in the selection process are significant, but fortunately easy to correct.

The bossy HR people who believe they are, among other things, *the* experts on selection, tell you that after years of 'research' they know the fundamental 'competencies' that are required for the job.

They can bang on endlessly about those competencies: They are the essential DNA of the company. It is the competency architecture that holds everything together. It prevents silos from forming. It links selection with training. It is a fundamental hallmark of the success of the company.

Ask for clarification – Where do these competencies come from? Are they born or made? Are there sex differences? – and you will be accused of effrontery. Are you challenging the experts? Do you want to destroy the company? And don't ask for any proof or indeed how one may prove that the competency list (for that is all it is) is comprehensive, clear, rank-ordered and essential for all jobs.

The interviewers are told that the competencies list is crucial. Their task is to gather enough good information to demonstrate that the candidate has (enough of) these competencies. They have to gather clear, sufficient behavioural evidence. The more evidence, the better; the more confidence the interviewer has in the candidate's competencies, the better.

Leaving aside the meaning of competencies, these are the three fundamental problems with this process:

1. *The idea that more is better.* Show you have lots (and lots) of the competency and you are in. But what do extreme scores mean? Extremes of normal are by definition abnormal. People who are very tall (over 6ft 8in) or short (less than 5ft) can have problems. But what about those who are really good at team work (they are dependent on their team); or really good with people (too soft, scared to confront poor performance); or serious, bright and analytic (too slow, too uncomfortable around ambiguity)?

   Are not great strengths often weaknesses? Are not strong preferences an indication of less flexibility? What has occurred to make a person have such an excess in one competency? Is it perhaps masking something else? Can a person chronically overuse a competency?

2. *The failure to identify sides to the candidate which you would not want in your organization.* This is called 'select out' as opposed to 'select in'. It is not the same as having enough of a competency. That leads to . . . yes, you guessed it . . . incompetency.

   Possessing an attitude that fits ill with the job can easily lead to derailment. What exactly are we talking about? Arrogance, paranoia, excessive emotionality. Those are known to be derailers, but they are surprisingly ignored, partly because they do not appear on the all-important competency list and partly because nobody has been given the job of identifying the 'select out' factors.

These select-out factors are known as the 'dark-side' variables. They are often related to psychiatric personality disorders and they are highly significant. Ignore them at your peril.

3. *Self-censorship*. A horrid combination of legal constraints and political correctness has led many selectors to fear asking the dark-side questions. There is an ever-growing list of 'no-no's' – age, religion, etc. – and there are those that seem just a bit 'too hot'. Imagine if you asked someone how religious they were, what age they were when they got married or how big their mortgage is.

'What', the soon-hired litigation lawyer wants to know, 'has that got to do with being a train guard or a sales assistant?' Well, often a great deal. If you travel through the various vocational guidance tests you may be surprised by the questions. Some have been derived from what is called the 'known groups' method. Suppose you found that all good tax inspectors played a lot of Monopoly as a child but no proven competent lawyer had done so, then you have a good selection question.

That is not the same as the two sides in the interview buying those clever-clever books on how to ask and how to answer smart-arsed questions. They are really about management skills, crucially important in certain jobs. This is something rather different. It is an attempt to pick up markers of job success.

You can ask about birth sign, birth order and colour preferences. That, however, probably (quite rightly) gives the impression that you are naïve, misinformed and have not read the literature. But what about: 'Were you a prefect at school?' 'What was your first job?' 'Describe anything entrepreneurial that you have ever done.'

The selection task is to attempt a good job fit. It means understanding the requirements of the job as well as the corporate culture. It means assessing the bright side of the individual: attitudes, beliefs, values, skills and personality . . . and it involves peering into the dark side, trying to see if there is anything there you don't want.

F. WRITING A PERSONAL STATEMENT

Apparently, prospective students really agonize about the 'personal statements' which are part of their university application form in the United Kingdom. It is an open page with few guidelines.

Parents, teachers and relatives are all called upon to provide wise counsel and even wiser words to ensure these statements bring about the desired outcome: namely the glittering prizes of acceptance to a great university. The question is all about the content and the style: how can you really impress the world-weary don sitting in their stuffy book-lined office?

The issue is so important that there is now a raft of companies that offer help and advice at £100–£300 a pop. There have been, as a consequence, outraged letters, inquiries and reports by various bodies into this wicked, underhand dissimulation. The concern is that it is a form of dishonesty that only the rich can buy. You pay a couple of hundred quid to get a place where you then need around £9000 a year just on tuition fees.

There are, however, three interesting issues here:

1. There is the naïve and taken-for-granted assumption that these personal statements actually play any part (at all) in the university selectors' decision-making. What evidence is there that they are even read, let alone factored into the selection process? Can anyone remember why they were put in the application form in the first place and by whom? Is there any empirical evidence whatsoever that the content of these statements relates to any aspect of the educational experience?

2. If, indeed, personal statements *are* considered, what factors are (most) important? Does evidence of helping little old ladies cross the road, or collecting money for the starving of Africa count more or less than (self-reported) evidence of being entrepreneurial, playing the violin to concert standard, or sporting achievements? Don't academics want people who are bright, hard-working and grown-up? Isn't that basically all? And if that is the case, how do you evidence those factors in your personal statement?

3. If personal statements are important, surely it is a positive sign that a student has sought advice from others. Is that not a sign of being a sensible adult? Surely the more assistance you receive from helpful teachers, parents and, yes, consultants, the better. And if you have personally earned the money and choose to spend it on a 'personal statement coach', should this not be rewarded and considered a sign of great things to come?

But what is the supposed function of a personal statement and why don't employers call for them? For the most part they could be regarded as a manifestation of impression management skills. For some they could equally be a manifestation of dissimilation (outright, blatant lies) or personal delusion (believing one's own propaganda). Certainly the aim is to impress. To show how worthy one is to be among the chosen.

Assuming they are an exercise in self-aggrandizement vs self-awareness, perhaps their usefulness is to judge them by those standards. Indeed, is not impression management a fundamental skill in all service jobs? Aren't all professionals, at least initially, in the impression management business? This suggests it is the image, not the reality, that is important.

So why don't big organizations copy the Universities and Colleges Admissions Service (UCAS) people and call for personal statements? True, some do, under the guise of those frustrating open-ended, empty box questions, such as: 'Why do you want this position?', 'What do you think you might bring to this particular job?' 'Why do you think you are particularly suited to working for us?' This makes an amusing exercise for those who believe they have a sort of quasi-psychoanalytic insight into the true nature of individuals. In the jargon they are called projective techniques, where the writer projects his/her deep-seated motives into the text.

One reason why employers *don't* ask for a personal statement from job applicants is that the adult version is currently a three- to four- sentence paragraph at the top of the CV (now missing crucial data such as age). The usual characterization is 'I am a proactive, passionate, productive team player . . . blah, blah, blah.' No weaknesses, only strengths; no doubts, only certainties; no details, only impressions.

Another reason is, of course, the interview. Very few British universities interview candidates these days. And if they do, it's a very small percentage of applicants. The significance of the skill of impression management is during face-to-face encounters, not in writing. Interestingly, those who are morally outraged if candidates obtain help with their personal statements seem quite happy for people to receive selection interview training, costing much more time and money.

The skill of showing your 'best side' at an interview to a critical selector (or even a famous professor) reveals social skills, maturity, vocabulary and resilience. That is what counts in life, not what is written on the CV.

So don't fret about personal statements. They are all the same now and correlate very little with the truth. Some academics collect statements much as they do exam howlers. They tend to become documented as early evidence of *narcissistic personality disorder* or *naïve personal delusions*.

PART II

Getting the Best Out of People

Most people can remember their first supervisory role, even if it was as a school prefect or sports team leader. They needed to make their team understand what is need to be done, help them to achieve those goals and give them feedback on how they were doing. The resilient manager knows that you need to keep an eye on three things as a manager: the task, the team morale and the long-term strategy . . . and that you need to get the best out of those you have selected.

Some managers just seem to have a knack of getting the best out of their team. They seem to inspire pride and trust, and ensure that all team members are happy to go that extra mile for the leader and the team as a whole. What is it these managers do? How to they motivate? How do they respond to the individual differences of the people in the team? How do they manage performance?

This is no mystery. There are no hidden secrets. But it takes skill and effort. And the good news is that it is a skill that can be learnt.

A. ABSENCE ANALYTICS

In some sectors, absence can account for around 5 per cent of direct payroll costs. It often has huge cost implications. That's usually a big number – often as much as shoplifting, shrinkage and other losses. So why don't many organizations even try to measure it and manage it effectively?

Is absence more rife in the public than the private sector? Why is it so high in big, perhaps overstaffed, organizations? Why don't self-employed people seem to get ill?

At a national level it has been estimated that the costs of absence exceed £25 billion per annum. At an individual level the costs include hiring replacement staff, increasing overtime, losing sales, missing deadlines and generally poor customer service.

Results from the CBI suggest that top organizations have on average 2–3 days absence per annum per employee, while for badly performing organizations it is 10–14 days. This is particularly problematic for lean-process, just-in-time management, or where suddenly absent staff (say, in a school or surgery) can cause major disruption.

But, it seems, fewer than half of employers monitor the incidence cause or cost of absenteeism for their organization. Nor do they have a target or a process to reduce it. Most don't even know, therefore, whether absenteeism is high or low compared to sector averages.

It may seem a bit too embarrassing to admit the problem. Some employers may be scared of trying to introduce a system which monitors such things.

One reason for the problem is that there seems to be no way and nobody to analyze the data on a spreadsheet. There are a range of possibilities for doing this: First, there is the clock-in method, given up by most companies years ago. Nowadays, there is the more insidious practice of using 'swipe' entry card data or desktop computer log-in as data. That is easy – it can be done under the guise of security and it works increasingly efficiently.

But the fact that the person has not come to work does not mean absenteeism. They could just as well be on holiday, working from home or at a meeting on a different site.

Computer log-in data, can of course, be collected anywhere, but also perhaps used as a smoke screen: the modern day equivalent of the 'jacket on the chair' trick.

The fact that someone is on-line can mean little or nothing about the work they are supposed to do. The question is: who then collects, interprets, and can act on this data? To many people it seems astonishing that this is neither implemented nor considered by HR to be a fundamental part of what they do.

Analysis of absenteeism can highlight all sorts of 'hot spots'. Why are some people so frequently absent? Why are the people in one department three times as likely to go absent as people in another? Why do people at Grade 4 (supervisors) go absent at eight times the rate of those at Grade 5 (junior managers)? And why do some individuals tend to have only the odd day off while others take whole weeks?

One reason why some organizations don't gather absenteeism data is because they don't really want to know. They also refuse staff surveys for the same reason. Of course they do know there's a problem and feel embarrassed but powerless. Absenteeism is a hot issue. What if you find women, ethnic minorities or young people have much higher absenteeism? The work–life balance mantra is soon chanted. You get lots of bad publicity. The issue is so sensitive that you are prepared to absorb the costs of normative absenteeism, which soon becomes culturally stabilized.

The causes of absenteeism are many: poor management, poorly designed systems and workloads, poor employee care programmes. So what's to be done? First, log the absenteeism data and let everyone see the results. Second, make it a supervisor/management issue, not (exclusively) an HR issue. Third, institute simple, subtle but random 'return-to-work' interviews. Fourth, consider how one could be more flexible in work scheduling. Fifth, hold organization-wide (all level) meetings to agree good absence management practices. And get the medical staff, the unions and everyone else involved.

There are other, more radical suggestions. Give people a 'no-claims bonus' for not being absent. A similar idea is the planned time-off concept where all days off (holidays, sick leave) are bundled together – easier to administrate but tough on the chronically ill, and, of course, illegal in many countries.

The bad news is that absenteeism is a sensitive marker of disengagement, which is usually a management issue. But there are other causes, such as working in declining industries, or staff cutbacks that exacerbate the problem.

It is no accident that so many public sector employers ask about absenteeism when requesting a reference. It's a big issue for the vast number of them who don't seem to manage the issue well.

And the bottom line? Somebody in the organization should have some decent stats on the cost of absenteeism. A relaunch can tighten up the attendance management practices. Reward individuals, managers and departments who are attending well and investigate those where things are not so hot. Don't get obsessed with 'presentism' because it may not relate to productivity.

B. EXPERIENTIAL INCENTIVES

Salespeople don't like doing paperwork. Period. Yes, a truism that's generally true. Their profile makes the post 'thrill of the kill' documentation a terrible bore. They are just not suited to sitting there with a laptop filling in all the (tedious) details of the sale they have just made.

This upsets the finance department who need the numbers on time, error-free and in their chosen format. So how to proceed? How to ensure that salespeople get into the habit of doing their figures correctly, on time and, possibly, even with pleasure?

Another truism: salespeople are competitive, 'flash' and very reward sensitive. They seem to value things others think daft, trivial and shallow – the conspicuous 'salesman of the month' parking space next to the chairman's, some daft set of trophies, perhaps an upgrade in their company car. Go to a sales conference and see the 'come on down' atmosphere as people are given numerous toys and trinkets as rewards. Sometimes they are given big(ish) cheques. Money, say the psychologists is a generalized reinforcer. But that can get very expensive. How do you get a relatively cheap but effective way of developing a good habit?

After a few false starts, one company that faced the problem found a solution. This had four component parts, each of them important. It went something like this: if a sales person got their sales data in to the finance quant-jocks (mathematically very talented people) sufficiently satisfactorily every month *for a year*, they and *their whole family*, would win a *fully paid holiday* in the Caribbean/Med/Indian Ocean.

The following were the four components involved in the success of this incentive scheme:

1. *The one-year aspect.* Why? Get employees into the habit. Postponement of gratification. This is behaviour change, not a short-term game. Diets don't work because they don't involve behaviour change. A change in lifestyle does. It is commitment to the long haul. Yes, more difficult, especially for impulsive, short-termist, quick-fix salespeople. But it was a serious prize.

2. *The prize was shared by the recipient's family.* This was most important for various reasons: It meant that the salesperson then came under domestic pressure to succeed. This could more accurately be described as support rather than pressure – just as all exercisers, dieters and lifestyle changers know the task is made easier if there is social support. Indeed, in some instances the family acted as educators, helping the less computer literate salesperson master the technology.

3. *Rewards can be materialistic or experiential.* This component was possibly the most significant. One school of thought – call them vulgar materialists – argues that it is much better to have something tangible. Certainly, we know that materialists derive happiness from signalling their wealth because this is how they measure success and define themselves and others. Purchases signal status. He who has the most toys is the winner.

   But if you ask people to describe themselves, the important markers in their life, or how others perceive them, they rarely say that their Rolex, Porsche or Prada bag sums them up. Paradoxically, experiments that are products of the service economy, not the manufacturing economy, are more valued over time. The materialists say a possession has resale value; it does not (necessarily) depreciate; it is an heirloom. But ask people what they would save from a burning house and it is more likely to be photographs or a scrapbook, not the family silver.

   We know that memories of powerful experiences become embellished. Rose-tinted spectacles make the experience better. They do so partly as a result of the richness and ambiguity of experiences over material goods. The holiday with bad weather may allow explorations off the beach. And experiences seem to serve higher-order goals.

   So the family holiday . . . the family is proud of the wage earner's achievement. Like stolen fruit, things taste better when free – in this case not only free but earned, won, deserved. You can return from a holiday tanned and relaxed. And so can the family. They can bask in the reflected glory. Photographs can be emailed. The news can spread. Compare this to a set of golf clubs or a cheque to be spent on a new TV set.

4. *All can become winners.* This is not a winner-takes-all system that causes resentment and even sabotage among competitors. If everybody fulfils the criteria,

everybody can win. Indeed, they may encourage one another to do the paperwork as required.

Ten family holidays – wouldn't that be preposterously expensive? The company looked into it and compared prices . . . vs the cost of a consultant led culture change programme . . . vs the cost of a one-off expensive present competition that had no long-term behaviour change and that needed to be repeated.

Don't underestimate the efficacy of experiential incentives. The psychotherapists know that experiences, not possessions, bring happiness. People look back and regret the things they did not do, rather than the things they did not buy.

Like good wine, experiences improve with time. Moths and rust corrupt, thieves break in and steal but memories are forever . . . particularly if they are shared and the result of a prize at work.

C. EXTROVERTS

Got their come uppance at last, heh? The hegemony of extroversion has been challenged. Noisy, shallow, attention-seeking extroverts are under attack at last. The end of bias and discrimination against innocent introverts?

The book *Quiet: The Power of Introverts* by Susan Cain has taken that most extroverted of nations, America, by storm. It is a sort of defence of introversion in a world seemingly dominated by extroverts. The author, who claimed it took her seven years to write the book (very introverted), has appeared on TED (high-quality, brief lectures by experts and available on the web (very extroverted behaviour)), no doubt because her agent told her to. Or because she is a well-adjusted, socialized introvert who knows you have to appear extroverted to get on in life.

Of course, people are not nicely divided into two types as the naïve enthusiasts of the neo-Jungian, Myers-Briggs

Type Indicator (MBTI) suppose. Introversion–extroversion is a dimension from very high to very low. It's a bit like height – people are neither tall nor short; some are, but most are not. So, most of us are *ambiverts* – in the middle; not strongly the one or the other. We can look at others both more introverted and more extroverted, depending on our situation. But it is easier talking about one type or the other, and people readily and happily put themselves on one side of the line. So, are you quiet introverts victimized by vacuous extroverts?

Extroverts are seen as more likeable, interesting and popular; introverts more honest, stable and reliable. Extroverts are attracted to 'people jobs' such as sales and the service industry, and do well. The stereotypic introvert is a librarian. Do all the sexy, well-paid jobs call for extroverts? Are introverts the children of a lesser God?

Cain, who is a cheerleader for introverts, maintains that the world likes extroverts because they favour action over contemplation. She advocates three things bring out the best from introverts in the workplace: stop group work and let people work on their own; let people go to 'the wilderness' where they can be themselves, think and contemplate; and 'open their suitcase', meaning allow them to explore things that interest them.

Americans are fond of the concept of bias, discrimination and stigma. The world values extroverts and their ways; introverts are discriminated against. Labelled as shy, slow, inadequate or dull, they lurk in the shadows while the extroverts hog the limelight.

So why is (or was) the world biased in favour of extroverts? Or is so much of modern work with relentless screen time, spreadsheets and data entry designed for introverts? Consider three factors:

1. *Extroverts are less distracted than introverts.* The world is ever more busy, noisy and distracting. The open-plan

office, the mobile phone and the relentless meetings all favour extroverts, who like stimulation. Introverts, on the other hand, just get distracted by people, noise, or stimulants of any kind. They are less comfortable, less efficient and less helpful when the world of work is noisy.

2. *The world is getting faster.* Introverts take longer to retrieve information, longer to marshal their ideas and thoughts and longer to respond to the demands of the world around them. Slow is bad.

3. *Extroverts respond better to carrots and care less about sticks.* Introverts, on the other hand, are less motivated by rewards and more sensitive to, and inhibited by, threats of punishments. Perhaps extroverts are easier to manage. They are certainly easier to read.

People like extroverts because they tend to be more socially confident and comfortable. Children move towards, away from, or against, people. The stimulus seeking extrovert learns early on that people can be lots of fun. So, most of them learn social and emotional intelligence earlier.

But there have always been serious known *disadvantages* of being a (strong) extrovert. Consider a few

Accidents: Extroverts are risk takers. They drive fast and choose risky recreational activities. They trade off accuracy for speed. They are prone to all sorts of gaffes, preferring to think before they speak.

Crime: Extroverts are social and impulsive. They are excitement-seekers, interested in novel experiences, which often leads them to be poorer learners than introverts at many tasks, including the acquisition of general social rules. They are difficult to train, naughty and rebellious. They are more likely than introverts to become delinquents or criminals, though it does depend on the nature of the criminal activity.

Learning: Extroverts do well at primary school but less well at university. The idea of sitting in a quiet room for hours, learning about complicated abstract ideas, just doesn't suit the extrovert.

Sex: Extroverts have obvious advantages above and below the duvet. They tend to be less prudish and nervous than their introverted cousins, and more excited and satisfied with sex. But extroverts are more likely to have premarital sex and more likely to experiment. They are prone to promiscuity . . . and they get caught.

But there is a serious caveat with all this stuff. Extroversion is but one dimension of personality and it interacts with other powerful factors. The neurotic, moody, unstable extrovert can be unattractively touchy, restless and aggressive, while the neurotic introvert may be over-anxious, rigid and pessimistic. Some introverts are more agreeable and more conscientious than others. Some are brighter than others and more creative.

Give me a bright, creative, empathic and hard-working person any time. And you can keep the dim, tough-minded, disorganized and feckless person, whatever the degree of introversion.

D. FACTS OF LIFE

Impressive chap, Bill Gates – self-made multi-billionaire, business and computer genius and, more recently, enthusiastic philanthropist. Made a lot . . . and giving lots away.

The stereotypic geek? Low emotional intelligence? Understands toys/computers/systems but not people? Hardly. There are many reasons to dispute this negative stereotype, not least of which is his history of building the company that made his fortune. You need more than product development to do that. Particularly in the early stages. You have to convince investors and co-workers, and motivate staff.

Perhaps the best evidence of the wisdom of Gates is the hugely popular, widely cited reality-check he gave to a high school graduation audience. It's difficult to verify exactly what was said because of the Chinese whispers nature of the web. It does not matter much; the points he (supposedly) made were direct, simple and true. They are clearly not politically correct and are against all the self-esteem movement ideas of 'blame-others' and all must have prizes.

It looks like a good dose of realistic, work ethic therapy. He tells secondary school children not to blame their teachers or parents for failure. Take responsibility – you, and you alone, are captain of your ship and master of your fate. Life is not fair – the rain falls on the just and the unjust alike. There are winners and losers in life. Working hard with the right attitude increases your chance of being a winner. Particularly the attitude-thing – this is pitching up and pitching in . . . and not phoning in sick when you just feel a tad tired after a night on the tiles.

Self-esteem building or therapy doesn't lead to success. Effort does. Success through effort and ability lead to people feeling justifiably proud. Not the other way around, where boasting your (limited) talent leads to success.

Learn to work and work hard – start at the bottom and work your way up, like your parents and grandparents did. Fast tracking is rare and becoming rarer. The long journey to the top teaches great lessons and skills.

School is, in many ways, a bad model for life. There are no long holidays or gap years in the adult world. There are no textbooks, TV/videogames and the rest to distort reality. Be grateful to your parents. And don't despise nerds (perhaps a self-reference) because they are likely to become your employers. Technical people have a lot to offer.

Wonderful stuff. Music to the ears of many middle-aged teachers worn down by the entitlement narcissism of young people over-fed with 'I am special' philosophy.

Using Gates' brilliant model, what would you say at an MBA graduation ceremony? How different the 28-year-old from the 18-year-old. Sure, they are probably smarter, definitely poorer (very temporarily), and clearly more tired than the school kid. But have they too been fed on a series of myths by business schools that are in ever greater competition with each other.

In 1965 there was one business school in Britain; now there are over 100 offering astonishing benefits for a *mere* £30K–£50K investment. The hidden message is this: To become a very well-paid high-flyer – one of the fast-streamed, talented group to be catapulted to success – you need this piece of paper. It costs a lot in terms of time and money. But it is a very good investment. It is a guarantee of really high returns. It's going to be a pretty miserable and stressful year or two. Perhaps a year out of your life. But you will make new friends, network with new and important people and have many windows of opportunity opened. You will be among the chosen, the elite, the super-rich.

So what to tell these graduates in the Bill Gates spirit of reality check? *Rule 1*: Nobody will really care whether you got your MBA from the University of Camford or North Neasden. They don't know or care much about all that ranking and rating stuff. *Rule 2*: Neither will they care if you were awarded a distinction, were on the Dean's list, or won a prize for the best essay in Entrepreneurial Psychology. *Rule 3*: Your attitude to work is more important than qualifications, and these very qualifications may have distorted your values, making you (paradoxically) less attractive. *Rule 4*: Business Schools and Universities are mostly state sector places that do not model good business practice. *Rule 5*: Ambition is nothing without hard work and talent. *Rule 6*: The exclusivity of having an MBA reduces every year. It is less and less of a competitive advantage. They are two-a-penny now. Try something else. *Rule 7*: The 'hard' courses (finance) are equally as important as the 'easy' courses (ethics). *Rule 8*: Leadership and management can't easily be taught in classrooms . . . like riding a bicycle, flying a helicopter, playing the violin, practice is more important than theory. You can't learn to lead from PowerPoint. *Rule 9*: The banker bonus world is finished. You will not be on £6K multiplied by your age and have a Lear Jet at the age of 40. Get real. *Rule 10*: Pay a price or suffer a cost. Who paid the greatest cost during your MBA year – partner, parents, children? It's time to pay them back.

E. FUDGING AND NUDGING

Changing public behaviour is enormously expensive and difficult. Every government would like to know how to get the public to drink and smoke less, exercise more, pay their taxes, eat more healthily, etc. It really is a holy grail. A knighthood in the bag if you can come up with a cheap(ish) and efficient solution.

There used to be only two ways to address this issue: *education* and *regulation*. Proponents of the two positions would often go head to head over very specific issues, such as alcohol, fizzy drinks or fast foods. In particular, television advertising and advertising to children got them going. Each side knew that they alone were right and the others were wrong.

It was often a left- vs right-wing, pro- vs anti-business tussle; companies vs the government; libertarians vs socialists. The educators said that you can influence people's eating and drinking habits by persuasive techniques, namely education; people should not be infantilized or nannied by the state. They particularly loathed the mountain of do-gooder 'behalfers' who claimed to speak on behalf of all 'concerned parents', 'lower-income groups' or 'the disadvantaged'.

Educators also criticized the naïve assumption that, for instance, television advertisements (to children) create 'false wants' and then children pester power their hapless parents into buying things they otherwise would not. The educators argue that it is parental values and lifestyle that influence a child's preferences and wants – how much television they watch and how much pocket money they are given.

Educators pointed out how little good research the regulators and protectionists had to support their position. They highlighted the educative role of television and the fact that advertising pays for programming. They often noted with glee how bans can backfire (remember prohibition) and that legislation subverted the family, nationalized children and reduced all sense of responsibility.

The legislators claim to have plenty of survey evidence to show that people want legislation and that it works. They point out that if advertising had little effect on sales it would not be used. They distrust the self-regulation of various sector bodies and want tough rules. Legislation covers what, and when, and how, things are advertised, priced and available. And it can escalate – see what is happening to cigarette marketing. Tax alcohol more, and people drink less. Amen.

There are other 'perks' to legislation and protectionism. It can yield some hefty tax income. Politicians are seen to be 'doing something' and they can take the moral high ground.

But there is now a new kid on the block. A new concept based on the sexy new science of *Behavioural Economics*. The concept is to *nudge*. It claims to be cheap, effective and not coercive. The psychobabble says that all you need do is *manipulate the choice architecture*. You have to rely on people's automatic, heuristic thinking. It's all based on the work of Daniel Kahneman, a psychologist who won the Nobel prize for economics. The idea is to change the environment, the package and the message, and people make different choices.

So with alcohol, the legislative approach is to tax more, restrict outlets, ban advertising; the educational approach is to run courses in schools and clubs for young people and persuade producers to follow a code. But nudges try something quite different: they let people know what average consumption looks like, and how many people do not drink at all so that they have some sense of comparison. They also encourage people to serve drinks in smaller glasses.

Nudging is really attractive to enlightened, libertarian paternalists. Give people some choice, but guide them in those choices and they will willingly and happily do what you want. Nudging is very cheap. So, inform people that most others like them in their area pay their full tax commitments and they will respond by reducing their attempts at avoidance or possible evasion.

But, you wisely say, it can't be that simple. Four questions: First, does it work in the long term? Is there evidence that one or more of these cheap interventions shows *sustained change in behaviour?* Second, is it really cost-effective? Third, do you need a whole fist of the nudges at the same time for anything significant to happen? And, finally, do you need to back up nudging with either or both education and/or legislation?

At this stage there is more absence of evidence than evidence of absence. There are some impressive small-scale studies published in academic journals that seem very promising. And there are plenty of consultants who have jumped on the bandwagon, telling you how to persuade people at very little cost. Sort of Vance Packard and the 'hidden persuaders' all over again.

There is also that old friend *unintended consequences*. Since nudging is not always very targeted, special groups who need it most might receive less attention than the average person.

But we still don't know when, for whom or how long nudging works. Make stairs more attractive and people will leap up them and not take the lift; design supermarket trolleys so that there are special prominent places for large fruit and veg to encourage people to choose a big trolley rather than a small basket.

So, is it better to be nudged, nannied or instructed? Is nudging a short-term fashionable gimmick? Time will tell.

F. HIRE EMOTIONALLY INTELLIGENT PEOPLE

The advent of positive psychology and the economists' shocking realization that money is only weakly related to well-being has led to a flurry of books on happiness.

The jury is still out with regard to teaching happiness. We all know the *heart-sinking* person, the pessimist, the complainer, the gloom-and-doom monger. Whatever happens to them, they remain negative, helpless and hopeless.

By contrast we know the *life-enhancers*. They may be called sunny or bonny or simply optimists. They bounce back from adversity and remain resolutely positive.

They are, for the most part, stable extroverts, while the heart-sinkers are unstable introverts. And there is not much to be done about one's personality. You are what you are. We know that people do not change much over time. We do become a little more neurotic and a little less extroverted, but these personality traits are remarkably stable despite what happens to us, be it winning the lottery or a terrible accident leaving us paralyzed.

But we can assess and improve *emotional intelligence*. People with more emotional intelligence are happier; they are more perceptive and sensitive to others; more rewarding and more fun; more adaptable and flexible. They find it easier to make and keep friends . . . a crucial ingredient for happiness.

Emotional intelligence is about being aware of, and sensitive to, one's own and other's moods. But it is also about the *management* of those moods. So, emotionally intelligent people are better at reading and shaping their own and others' moods – a key ingredient of success.

And studies of personality, emotion and mood in the workplace have found, not surprisingly, that happy people (simply defined as those who experience positive emotions) are more successful. Compared to unhappy people, but matched on other criteria such as education, experience, skills:

- Happier people find better jobs – with more autonomy, variety and meaning.
- Happier CEOs have happier people working for them.
- Happier people show better job performance.
- Happier people make more money.

These findings hold true across jobs from counsellors to cricketers and in different countries from German industrialists to Malaysian farmers.

So what explains these findings? Why is there a connection between positive moods, a sense of well-being, happiness and work success? There seem to be several different factors:

Focus and distraction: Unhappy people are too prone to taking their eye off the ball at work. They tend to be more self-obsessed and not as vigilant about the needs of others, be they colleagues or customers. Emotional intelligence teaches one to be more 'other' focused.

Memory: The mood-conjuring effect is well established. People in a good mood recall more positive things and vice versa. Hence we get virtuous and vicious cycles. Positive people recall happy customers and co-operative peers; unhappy people never let go off their negative experiences. Positive people put in more effort to achieve the positive results they will recall.

Decision-making: People with sunny dispositions make better decisions: they are faster, more accurate and more inclusive. Unhappy people are too 'hung up' about small, irrelevant issues and alienate those who are trying to help them. Optimistic people believe that problems are solvable and that they can (with help) make good decisions. The pessimists are energy sapping and often either procrastinate or make poorer decisions than the optimists.

Evaluating others: We all know that bosses are best avoided when they are in a bad mood, particularly for annual appraisals. People in a good mood are more encouraging, more forgiving, and more tolerant of others and their 'little foibles'. Negative moods are associated with blaming and attacking others, rather than helping them. Negative people make bad colleagues and team members.

Co-operating: Good moods make people more generous, more co-operative, more helpful. People in a good mood tend to deflate crises and resolve conflicts. Those in a bad mood increase conflict.

No one likes an unpredictable, moody boss, colleague or customer. This instability is called 'neuroticism' and is associated with anxiety, depression, and hypochondriasis. We also shy away from people who shy away from us. This is called introversion. We quite happily use personality tests in selection, so why not use them to 'select-in' dispositionally happy people and 'select out' unhappy people? Should optimism be a competency?

Management is a contact sport. We can all, irrespective of our personality, learn to improve our social and interpersonal skills and in the process become emotionally intelligent.

The happiness gurus give this advice: Accept that enduring happiness doesn't come from worldly and materialistic success. Take control of your time, aim for a little progress each day. Act happy, because going through the motions can trigger the emotions you need. Seek work and leisure that engages your natural strengths and skills. Join social groups that reflect your interests, values and passions. Get enough exercise and sleep every day. Give priority to close relationships, by affirming others and sharing together. Focus on others more than yourself. Keep a record of good things that happened to you (gifts, blessings).

They should also have added: Improve your emotional intelligence. Other people are by far the best source of well-being. Give what you want to receive. Remember, we are people of the head and heart . . . and they are connected.

G. MID-LEVEL CADRES

Teaching assistants, community support officers, nursing auxiliaries. The idea of *task shifting* jobs, where a number of very specific tasks can be reallocated from more to less specialized personnel, appears to have taken hold.

Is this a cynical or cash-strapped government trying to save money? Or one that is trying to create jobs? What is the evidence for their efficacy? Are there fewer crimes where community support officers operate? Or is the aim to make people feel more secure as they see more uniformed people about? That is, crime levels remain the same but *fear of crime* is reduced. Do real police persons then get on with the 'real' job of policing? And if so, how is the 'real' job defined.

What jobs don't lend themselves to the development of mid-level cadres? Brain surgeons, aircraft pilots, nuclear submariners? Of course, all these professionals are supported by assistants who (often) have less training, but the professionals alone are entrusted with the major tasks and decisions.

But how to determine the 'task shifting'? It appears to have been driven more by service needs than by a serious job analysis, skill-set specification or consideration of educational/capacity levels.

A major reason for resistance is that this analysis highlights where the real expertise lies. It demands that skills are put into a hierarchy which may be difficult to define.

The issue of professionalization, particularly in the medical area, has fascinated sociologists for some time. What is the skill level difference between a midwife, a senior midwife, a junior obstetrician and a senior obstetrician? Is it a matter of training, expertise and skill? Do they have different specialism approaches – ideologies which are essentially complementary? Do some have more legal power and authority than others? But, more importantly, what happens to these job categories over time?

One of the interesting and important issues for job splitting is whether, as a customer, one is passed up or down the chain. So, in medicine it is likely that patients might be seen by a practice nurse who does a quick assessment (triage) of who needs to see the doctor or not. And the doctor – a GP – may make the same decision about referring a patient to a specialist, or not.

What are the problems associated with task-shifting? It seems to take years for the process to settle down so that both (or more) groups are happy with their lot. Is it really about status and identity?

Perhaps performance management systems (PMS) that insist on performance measurement have in part fuelled the trend for task splitting and shifting. The performance measurement people argue that for fairness and equity at work which is manifest in performance related pay, it is crucial to promote and reward the most able and targeted training. They argue that we need to measure all salient behaviour at work.

So how to measure teachers? By the grades of their pupils or the happiness of the students? What if it is shown that however well pupils did in a subject, none ever went on to study the subject at university? Or that pupils became so burnt out in their high-grade pursuit that they never wanted to repeat the experience again? That is, the pursuit of the extrinsic rewards (grades) comes at the cost of the intrinsic rewards (the pleasure of learning).

Performance measurement means data – usually forms. And so, we hear, doctors and the police spend too much of their time in (seemingly pointless) bureaucratic work, and not enough time getting on with their real job of curing patients and preventing/solving crimes. So mid-level cadres are provided to do these onerous tasks and let the real professionals get on with the real job.

Top executives have *personal assistants*, though the terms may have changed. Most often the CEO is a man and the PA a woman. Her task is to organize, plan and smooth the journey for the 'great man'. He, of course, carries the great burden of decision-making as well as building and maintaining a high-performance team . . . blah, blah . . . while she books rooms and flights, takes notes, buys presents, etc.

This goes way beyond secretarial duties; indeed, the PA may have a secretary or a PA. She is very powerful because she is privy to many secrets. Investigative journalists know this. As do airlines and hotels, who often try to influence the choices of airlines and venues by 'gifts' of one sort or another.

The task distribution or shifting often seems to boil down to the old task vs socio-emotional distinction. Someone does strategy, production and goal setting and another person does team building, morale and job satisfaction. Hard skills vs soft skills. Technical knowledge vs people skills. Product design, development and marketing vs customer relations, PR and staff engagement.

One gesture of task shifting is to consider lower-order, mid-level cadres essentially in charge of two things. First, getting the tools of the trade ready for the top bods: classrooms prepared for teachers, operating theatres for surgeons, files for barristers. Second, the jolly interpersonals to keep everyone happy.

Perhaps it is the latter point that is at the heart of this stuff. Professionals are trained in the theories, skills and attitudes of their profession. They are reasonably easy to define, specify and measure. They are seen to be at the heart of the work. These are the 'hard' skills. The soft skills – communication skills, social intelligence, motivational ability – seem relatively unimportant and it may be assumed that they are 'picked up' on the way. They become more important at the top levels of an organization and become more difficult to assess, define and measure.

The hard-bitten, tough executive can 'outsource' charm to his PA if he is lucky. It is not that clear if nurses can outsource this to auxiliaries or teachers to their assistants.

Somehow the soft stuff and the client contact skills seem to be given to mid-level cadres. And yet we know that this may make all the difference to the job in the end.

H. MOTIVATING YOUR STAFF

Most people have heard of only a few psychologists. One of these is *Sigmund Freud*, whom they often consider somewhere between a madman and a sex maniac. They also know about *Abraham Maslow* and his dreary, over simple 'theory' of job motivation. A few also know of *Frederick Herzberg*, who is remembered for his two-factor theory of job satisfaction: and the line they recall is 'money is a hygiene factor'. That's about it!

Herzberg, made sense of the many factors that influenced job satisfaction. In 1968, the year before we reached the moon, he published an article which has literally sold millions of copies. It was entitled *'One More Time, How Do You Motivate Employees?'* Its popularity is due to two things: first, it is the topic that exercises nearly all managers at work, and second, it is well written – succinct, simple and with practical implications.

Based on various interviews, Herzberg divided all the supposedly important factors influencing job satisfaction (autonomy, environment, training, salary, etc.) into two distinct factors. The theory goes like this. Some things at work only *prevent* dissatisfaction while others *encourage* satisfaction, but of course you need *both*. The former were called *hygiene factors* and the latter *motivators*. Now they tend to be called *extrinsic and intrinsic motivators*.

Extrinsic needs were said to be satisfied by the level of certain conditions (the *hygiene factors* or *dissatisfiers*). The factors that Herzberg found to be related to hygiene needs are: supervision style, interpersonal relations, physical working conditions, salary, company policies and administrative practices, benefits and job security. These factors are all concerned with the *context* or *environment* in which the job has to be done. When these factors are unfavourable, job dissatisfaction is the result.

Conversely, when hygiene factors are positive, such as when workers perceive that their pay is fair and that their working conditions are good, barriers to job satisfaction are removed. However, the fulfilment of hygiene needs cannot by itself result in job satisfaction, but only in the *reduction* or elimination of *dissatisfaction*. Herzberg compared hygiene factors to modern water- and air-pollution controls. Although such controls do not cure any diseases, they serve to *prevent* the outbreak of disease. In the same way, he and his colleagues believed that hygiene factors did not cause satisfaction, but that they could prevent dissatisfaction.

Unlike extrinsic needs, intrinsic needs are fulfiled by so-called *motivator factors* or *satisfiers*. These are achievement, recognition, work itself, responsibility and advancement. Whereas *hygiene* factors are related to the *context* of work, *motivator* factors are concerned with the *nature* of the work itself and the consequences of work. According to the theory, the factors that lead to job satisfaction are those that satisfy an individual's need for self-actualization (self-fulfilment) in their work, and it is only from the performance of the task that individuals can enjoy the rewards that will reinforce their aspirations. Compared to hygiene factors, which result in a 'neutral state' (neither satisfied nor dissatisfied), when present, positive motivator factors result in job satisfaction. When recognition, responsibility and other motivators are absent from a job, however, the result will not be dissatisfaction, as with the absence of hygiene factors, but rather the same neutral state associated with the *presence* of hygiene factors.

People are made dissatisfied by a poor physical environment, but they are seldom made satisfied by a good environment (i.e. don't believe architects when they talk about 'motivating environments'). The prevention of dissatisfaction is just as important as encouragement of motivator satisfaction. You need both sets of factors present. But hygiene and motivator factors are unrelated and independent. An individual can be highly motivated in his work and be dissatisfied with his work environment. All hygiene factors are equally important, although their frequency of occurrence differs considerably. Hygiene improvements have short-term effects (e.g. the positive effect of a pay rise soon disappears).

Attractive though the theory is, it has little empirical support. Researchers since the 1970s who have tried to replicate Herzberg's findings have shown that both types of factor can lead to either satisfaction or dissatisfaction. Further, the theory says nothing about individual differences: some people may be strongly in favour of job enrichment and others strongly against it.

Herzberg recommended *job enrichment* (and by implication job satisfaction), defined as an attempt by management to design tasks in such a way as to build in the opportunity for personal achievement, recognition, challenge and individual growth. It provides workers with more responsibility and autonomy in carrying out a complete task, and with timely feedback on their performance. Job enrichment consists of several measures such as removing controls from a job while retaining accountability – motivation by responsibility. It included giving each person a complete and natural module of work – motivation by achievement. Enrichment meant granting job freedom for a person's own work – motivation by responsibility, achievement and recognition. It also implied giving timely feedback on performance to the worker instead of to the supervisor – motivation by recognition. Real enrichment means introducing new tasks not previously performed – motivation by growth and learning. And it means assigning specific tasks so the employee can develop expertise in performing them – again motivation by responsibility, achievement and recognition.

There's still some good common sense in Herzberg. But he assumed satisfaction causes productivity, and therein lies the rub. Current research shows it may just as easily be the other way around.

I. PERFORMANCE APPRAISAL SYSTEMS

Performance appraisal systems: pointless paper chase or powerful motivational tool? Most people in the public sector, and many in the private, are deeply sceptical and cynical about performance appraisal. They have seen HR departments chop and change 'the form' endlessly, been on various workshops, filled in staff surveys . . . and still receive perfunctory appraisals and an apology for performance-related pay.

PMS are a powerful tool of change. They were used in the 1980s and 1990s to try to change the whole public sector culture and ethos. There are profound value differences between the old *service culture* and the new *performance culture*.

The service culture was based on the principle of experience and equality. People in the same job with the same experience (and qualifications) expected and got the same pay and had roughly the same prospects of promotion. In the process of 'doing one's time', one gained experience, showed loyalty and commitment, and learnt the corporate culture. You waited for your turn.

People were paid equally for equal work . . . or at least for being in the same job. The unions liked that and bargained and negotiated for pay for specific levels. Annual appraisals were not taken seriously and often not done at all . . . there was not much point.

And then the new ethic came along. This was based on equity not equality, and the new word was performance. You get rewarded for what you do, and you need help and clear feedback on a regular basis from your boss on how you are doing. You need specific goals and targets with measurable success criteria (KRAs, KPIs), regular progress reviews and a meaningful annual appraisal. Data have to be collected on performance and these serve the basis for all decision-making. Radical stuff.

It has been known for 80 years that (by and large) the best worker produces about two-and-a-half times as much as the least productive worker. The equity principle says that input should relate equitable to output, and therefore every worker's 'reward package' should be directly related to his/her productivity.

Therefore, and here's the tough bit, two people in the same job and with the same experience should not be paid the same unless their productivity is the same. Equal pay was only fair if there was equal output . . . and patently there was not. And equally important it meant really *measuring output*. You cannot manage what you do not measure . . . as the new mantra went.

Many people in the public sector were aghast. Their currency was now useless. It did not matter how long they had served . . . it was all about their productivity, which was now subject to measurement. Not only were years of service deemed irrelevant (and sometimes even pitiable), but they now felt under surveillance.

Once the new system was explained, the most common reaction (after shock, horror and anger) was to explain that it seemed a good idea, *but for others*. 'You see', the old-fashioned public sector employee explained (patronizingly), '*our* output cannot be measured.' How do you measure the output of a nurse, or a social worker, or a policeman or a university teacher? Impossible . . . and therefore (alas) we cannot use the system.

So the PMS supporters enquired how organizations made decisions about promotion, training, etc . . . was it based only on time serving? 'No, of course not,' came the defence, 'it is based on performance!' But how is that measured/assessed? Silence.

In the brave days of the 1980s when Thatcherism was an unstoppable force, many public bodies were cajoled into reworking their PMS and experimented with an equitable pay-for-performance system. Needless to say, it was strongly resisted at various levels. It is not difficult to sabotage these systems and this was done.

The problem lay not so much in measuring performance, though that is not easy, but in the inequitable reward. What does an organization do if it shows that the best employees do two-and-a-half times as much as the worst? Pay them two-and-a-half times as much perhaps.

Chaos, disenchantment and resistance led to revision of the system. The measurement was kept and the appraisals had to be done, and the (damn) forms filled out. But the performance-related reward bit was fudged. The difference between the top award and the bottom was very small (often a couple of hundred pounds). So the principle of equity was creeping back to the old principle of equality.

But now no one was happy. All the bureaucracy remained: you have to get trained to do appraisals, you have to prove you have done them, you have to fill out the form . . . but it seems to have few consequences. Further, the worst employees remain jealous and the best are demotivated because the promise was not kept.

This is where many of us are today. This is the 'third way' of performance appraisal.

So what to do? Everyone needs some idea of what their manager wants from them (goals), they need feedback on how they are doing (appraisals) and they need to be rewarded for their effort. That is common sense. The hard bit is the reward and whether it is equitable.

J. PROMOTE AT RANDOM

It is always fun (for some at least) when cherished ideas and orthodoxies are challenged by the results of evidence-based studies. The evidence-based concept has caused frustration and consternation in many branches of activity, especially medicine, where long-held notions and practices have been found to be quite useless, even dangerous. The evidence-based theories are, however, now spreading to that woolly (at best) social science – 'management studies'.

Back in 1984, *The Economist* invited finance ministers, company chairmen, Oxford students and dustmen to give a 10-year view on the economy. They had a nice measured outcome. And, yes, you guessed it . . .

There have also been some intriguing studies on promotion at work. We all assume that, through careful data analysis and wise decision-making, those most able and deserving are promoted (over others) to top-ranking positions. But this is self-evidently not true if you have some life experience of senior managers.

Ask any group to describe in detail the characteristics of various bad bosses they have had and you will generate flipcharts covered in behaviours and types: bullies and bastards, deviants and dullards, narcissists and nay-sayers. It seems for many a deeply cathartic exercise to offload their frustrations with a promotion procedure that was clearly at fault. Yet those who have been around a bit know that this is not quite right. Consider the options:

Buggins' turn: This can take many forms but is more about time served rather than performance. Keep your head down, your powder dry, don't rock the boat, and in due course you will be promoted. No doubt until you prove to be completely incompetent.

Have-a-go: This is the 'live and die by the sword' style of management. The idea is that quite early on in your career you are given serious responsibilities. Everyone has a chance . . . if they want it. If you succeed, you stay; if you fail, you go. Up or out. Darwinian: survival of the fittest, fastest, fattest.

Cabals: All organizations have their insiders and outsiders. The chosen group may be linked together for a host of reasons, be it ideology or past experience, and they look after each other. People who share school or university, city or region, and interests or passions form groups which help each other. You have to be a cabal member in order to be promoted.

HR metrics: There are supposedly reliable scientific methods for finding those most suited to senior jobs. There are assessment centres, judgements of psychologists, stretch assignments, and so on that people can be put through to test their mettle. Lots of judges, lots of tasks, lots of data. And those judged to be the best become the chosen.

But there is another method. And it has been tried by at least two groups of researchers – one American, the other Italian. It is the idea of promoting people *at random*! Yes, names in the hat, lucky draw. Those researchers were using the random method as a control group or even as the worst possible method they could think of.

Yet, to their surprise, the randomly promoted people did better than almost all other alternatives. Of course this caused consternation . . . and further research. And the suggestion was then to choose at random those who made the promotion decisions. So you could try a panel of people randomly entering the office at say 08.30 – a cleaner, two admin staff, three junior managers from one section and a bewildered customer.

If this observation is true – that randomizing is at least no worse than other methods – the question is: why? Presumably, the first issue is: who wants promotion and why? Not everyone seeks to climb the greasy pole. Sure, there are rewards: money, power, influence, but also stress! Perhaps many promotion drives are unhealthy and egocentric. They are all about what the organization can do for me rather than what I can do for the organization. So the paradox is that those who most want the promotion are the least appropriate for it.

Then there is the social mobility issue so beloved of the red team in Parliament. Some people choose their parents well. Their benefit is a good education, experiential opportunities of all kinds and a helping hand, often to get a job. Others, perhaps equally as able or even more able, miss out on so much. They lower their expectations, don't expect promotion and often don't get it. And the random method finds them.

Next, it is possible that good leadership is not that difficult. It seems reasonable to define leadership as the ability to direct and motivate a team better than its competitors. It is not clear that an MBA, or a proven list of competencies, is required for that. Some men discover it is harder running a toddler's party than a big company. Similar skills perhaps, but the former is far more testing.

Clearly, the random method has its limitations. First, those people who are randomly chosen should be asked if they want the job. No good if they don't. Second, they should be given a chance, but also some deadline/test to prove their worth. Third, they need support.

But boy, imagine the reactions of those people who are happy with the present system. Who have spent all their lives ducking and diving, charming and brown-nosing, bribing and bullying to get on the shortlist to the top. Consider the consternation and fury. The shock of all that wasted time and investment as someone who has quietly and efficiently got on with the job overtakes them to the corner office.

Suddenly demotivating, or surprisingly motivating? After all, life is a lottery. 'No man knows the hour' and all that. So scrap the succession management team, sack the assessment centre consultant and roll the dice. And come on down Mr Chairman.

K. PROMOTION OF THE SELF-AWARE

There are only two fundamental questions for the succession planners: Is s/he 'up *to* it' and 'up *for* it'? The questions are about ability *and* motivation. Can s/he do the job (well) and does s/he really want it? A little doubt raised by either answer merits serious investigation.

Most people are eager for the trappings and rewards of promotion: bigger salary, car, office, fancy title, etc... but are they prepared to take the stress and pressure of the challenges that leadership involves?

A problem with succession planning and, indeed, a lot of selection is that some jobs change both significantly and quickly over time. The skills and knowledge, as well as the attitudes and values, that seem to predict success in the job now may simply not apply in a few years as competition, technology and customer demands change. And it is not only that jobs change, but there is a world of difference between having a highly skilled job and managing highly skilled workers.

To have an eye for a person's supervisory and strategic abilities may be a really good thing. Indeed to be simple minded there are only three types of jobs: technical, supervisory and strategic. You are hired for your technical, job-relevant knowledge and skill. Some may take years to obtain and for that you pay a lot. But the next step up is supervision and management and the application of very different skills. If you're good at that, you may be allowed to join the grown-ups and do strategy.

Some aptitudes work for all jobs: emotional intelligence, the capacity to learn fast and efficiently, negotiation skills, stress tolerance, etc., but others may be very job specific. The ideal job is where the job demands are matched by the individual's capacity to fulfil those demands easily and happily.

The up-to-it/up-for-it game yields a very simple 2x2 matrix based on yes and no. Candidates who score 'yes' for both questions, or 'no' for both, are straightforward: the person wants the job and can do it, or they don't want it (thankfully) because they are judged essentially not able to do it.

But consider the other two options and what they might mean: The first is *can do it but doesn't want it*. Presuming it is a prestigious and well-paid promotion, why does the individual not 'rise to the challenge', 'grasp this (wonderful) opportunity', 'jump at it'?

There may be many reasons. First, a simple cost-benefit analysis. Though they have the capacity, skills and strength to do the job, they may decide that the stress, the political fighting or the time involved is not worth it. The difference in reward is not concomitant with the increased personal cost.

It could be that they have a rich or demanding set of commitments outside work – family, hobbies, particular passions. Some gurus – always men – seem to think the only fulfilment in life comes from work, with rewards such as seniority, bonuses and power over others. To their surprise, not all take this line. People may be very happy where they are – content. Lower level means more contentment, not less.

It could be a self-confidence issue. That is, colleagues and superiors are convinced the person is up to the job, but the individual in question is not. This may be a deeply ingrained humility, or a poor self-appraisal of inherent abilities. It may prove an interesting and important challenge for others.

But the real problem in this little 2×2 game is the person who is *up for it, but not really up to it.* Assuming the diagnosis is correct – that is, they don't have the capability – the question is what to do.

We have all met people who believe they are pretty special (and we have probably been through such a phase ourselves). Fed by all the high self-esteem, 'everyone is talented' (in their own special way), 'all must have prizes' nonsense. Some (dare one admit) young people react with narcissistic rage when faced with rejection.

Told they do not have the maturity, the ability or wisdom for the role – that is, they are essentially not up to it – you may get an amazing temper tantrum. Fury, sulking, threats.

The question is: whence the poor self-evaluation. Why do they overrate themselves in comparison to (all) others. Possibly it is immaturity, a phase they are passing through. It may improve – some people grow up but others don't.

This essential lack of awareness may, however, hide something more serious. Over-estimating ability and motivation may be a sign of low social intelligence: the inability to observe others. It could even be due to low intelligence.

Self-awareness comes from two sources. First, seeking and accepting feedback from others. If everyone tends to say the same thing, it is clearly more than just churlish not to agree. Some block out feedback they don't like. Second, self-awareness comes from self-disclosure – from telling other people stuff and seeing how they react.

Being up for it, but not up to it can inspire action: to gain more experience or qualifications, to change habits, to change self-perceptions. It happens to most people at some point in their lives, and rejection can be a useful growth experience.

L. RANKING AND SPANKING

Okay then, hands up everyone who believes their organization has a good appraisal system. Anyone had a good experience of performance management? Is it 'a cynical charade where appraiser and appraisee conspire to complete what both see as pointless form filling'?

You can't really manage people without giving them direction and feedback. Set their goals, assist them in achieving these and give them a sense of how they are doing. Amen. This is the essence of good management. Most managers can (well, sort of) set clear (maybe unrealistic, unobtainable) goals and targets. Some understand they need to be supportive (sometimes). But few are any good at feedback – though most think they do it the whole time.

Appraisals are meant to standardize the feedback process. As HR sometimes say, it's an attempt to get managers who can't or won't actually manage. All very well having the power, glory and salary of management, but there are some requirements. Mandatory ones, not elective. And that is to give people timely, specific, actionable feedback on how they are doing. Yeah, yeah, yeah.

Easy, even enjoyable, to give the competent, hardworking employee positive feedback. Well done, here's the bonus, keep at it. But it's the slackers who cause the problems. And some organizations have their fair share of under-performers.

The question is how you give feedback – not whether it is verbal vs written, but how you score the individual. Some companies generate metrics, such as sales made per sales call, absenteeism and turnover, profit and revenue generated. You only have to chat to a group of adults from various professions to learn with some surprise that, for different reasons, their organizations seem unable or unwilling to gather any form of 'objective' behavioural data. As a consequence, they are forced to have managers/supervisors perform some kind of staff performance rating. This traditionally takes the form of statements about performance on a competency with a rating scale alongside. Thus, the supervisor has to rate the individual on 'shows initiative', 'always demonstrates exemplary customer interaction skills', 'is able to motivate their team'.

Pedants, purists and practitioners can have a field day fiddling about with those statements to make them fair, clear, relevant, etc. For the psychometrician, the issue is all about 'floor and ceiling' effects – that is, if everyone marks low or high, the rating has no differentiating value. Beware using the term discriminating.

Once you have the rating criteria, you need the scale. Is it 1–3 (i.e. an uneven scale) or 1–10 even? Should you have labels, from 1 = under-performance (or poor performance) to 10 = exemplary performance?

Organizations soon realize the problems with ratings: They are threefold:

1. A five-point scale soon becomes a three-point scale because no one uses the extreme scores. There is therefore little differentiation.
2. Organizations seem uncomfortable with eight- or ten-point scales because they are unable to come up with enough descriptive labels for performance. So, you have 'very poor', 'poor', 'average', 'good', 'very good', 'very, very good' and 'totally marvellous'.

3. You have characteristic rating styles. There is *manager softy*, who can't do tough love and confront poor performance. Conflict avoidant, balls-and-skill-less, he (for it is always a he) gives everybody high marks, thus making the really good resentful and the really poor complacent. Next, there is *manager midway*, who thinks everybody *is average*. Average at everything, all the time. So, he or she gives essentially the same scores to everybody and nobody receives any real feedback. Rarest is *manager nasty*, who rates everybody as helpless, hapless and hopeless.

The response of *some HR* departments has been to try ranking their staff. This comes in various guises. *The bell curve* – top 10 per cent, bottom 20 per cent, middle 70 per cent, or totem pole – top performer to worst performer. Or *quartiles* – first to fourth. Most know the famous Jack Welch Rank and Yank approach where, allegedly, the bottom 10 per cent are sacked every year, so driving up average performance.

There are arguments for forced ranking. It does identify top talent. It usually stops 'appraisal inflation'. It can reduce complacency and favouritism. It produces an up-or-out, perform-or-push-off culture. It certainly makes the performance management process as a whole more salient and relevant. And it's easier to link pay to performance by this method.

Software systems make ranking easy. General Electric story of economic recovery and success under the famous Jack Welsh.

But beware. There are distribution assumptions of bell-curve or ranking procedures. The bottom-ranked person in a very successful unit is still comparatively very good. Next, there is no reason to assume that the top person in finance is the same on all criteria as the top person in marketing. And the difference between those ranked 1 and 2 may be quite different from those ranked 4 and 5.

Then there are the long shadows of legal challenges. Can the ranker provide good evidence for a ranking that may seem to pick on minority groups?

Unsurprisingly, managers don't like the ranking system – particularly if the performance criteria for ranking that they are given doesn't fit with their experience. And for employees it is hardly the best thing for fostering team work.

Also rank and yank approaches seem to have a short life. A couple of years at most. After that you can be cutting lean flesh, not the fat.

Rating doesn't work then, nor does ranking . . . or perhaps they can with thought and training. But whatever you do, don't retreat into that slippery world of written descriptions without numbers. What precisely is 'satisfactory' performance – 4/10, 6/10 or what? How about 'must try harder' or 'works entirely to his own standards'?

Oh dear, no easy answers then . . . except train people to use well-thought-through, clear rating scales and to get themselves evaluated on those ratings.

M. SCIENTIFIC UNDERSTANDING OF THE PUBLIC

The most famous atheist of our time, Richard Dawkins, held a university chair in the *Public Understanding of Science*. Others have copied this clever idea, so there are professors of the Public Understanding of Psychiatry, Psychology and the Media. It's all about determining the public's lamentable knowledge about some subject and then educating them.

It is not difficult to demonstrate the public's ignorance, prejudice and stereotypic beliefs about any issue, from how things (the body, cars, medicine) work to knowledge of their history. Media '*vox pop*' interviews show how inarticulate and bewildered many people appear to be when faced with direct knowledge questions.

This is perhaps why there are so many charities – often started as self-help or support groups – whose task, as they see it, is to better inform the public about some issue, often a mental illness or handicap. They tend to follow a pattern: First, the shocking statistic about how many are there who 'suffer' from the problem. Second, how many famous people have had it. Third, how much 'sufferers' can, have and will achieve, in spite of their problem. And, finally, ways the unafflicted can help – especially by putting their hands in their pockets. There may also be a quiz to demonstrate the reader's ignorance, and how many myths they hold about a subject.

The research endeavour is all aimed at education. Hence, the borrowing of the much used concept of 'literacy'. So we have 'economic literacy' and 'media literacy'. The former is understanding how business and money works, the latter how to critique the media. Psychiatric literacy is about understanding the cause, manifestation and cure of mental illness.

Now every group wants their own particular literacy put on the school agenda. Some believe that happiness can be taught, so we have 'happiness literacy', while others believe students could do with a good shot of 'shopping literacy'.

One fun activity is to psychographically typologize the public into groups. It's a favourite journalistic activity: come up with amusing types graphically illustrated by a cartoonist. The 'know-all' who, of course, knows nothing and the 'bigot' who believes all the myths and prejudices. Good column but often bad science. The message, however, is an important one. 'The public' is not a single entity. People's knowledge and beliefs do indeed differ according to their age, class, sex, region and religion.

But there is another completely different set of researchers altogether. They are not so interested in what the public knows but what they do. The aim is to influence their behaviour. This is the *scientific understanding of the public.* They need to be housed in the ministry of propaganda. They were the ones who were responsible for the most tedious of all announcements and advertisements, namely *public service announcements.* Things like 'lock up the house when you leave it', 'turn the lights out' . . . very 'make do and mend', wartime stuff.

The scientific understanding of the public seems a lot more relevant and difficult than the public understanding of science. At the heart of all sales and marketing is the attempt to understand people's behaviour. A scientific understanding? Perhaps a social science understanding – a sort of 'lite science'. Marketing is about persuasion. It is an attempt to get the public to remember, buy or switch brands. The question is how to do it.

Does the old joke 'about half of all advertising works but no one knows which half' still apply? Not so much. There are a number of established facts in the world of advertising and marketing. Some techniques work better than others. Amen. The problem lies in all the strange awards which arty-farty types like to give each other. Like plays reviewed by bored theatre critics who have seen Hamlet 100 times and love the nude version set in a 1950's theme-park, advertisements are often commended for their dramatic impact, use of sound, colour and surprise. In many it is not even clear what is being advertised.

But it is not only sales and marketing that need a good shot of social science. More than anyone it should be HR, now renamed 'The Talent Group'. They, after all, advise about selection and pay. They demand appraisals and exit interviews. Required processes and practices stream from their emails: restricting, taxing and frustrating people at every turn. The question is the evidence base: *the scientific understanding of the worker.* Is there any scientific evidence to support all those oft-repeated catchphrases about engagement leading to profitability, emotional intelligence being more important than IQ?

We do know that people need stretching goals and targets, feedback on how they are doing, and support. We can be more specific about each of these factors: the clarity of goals, the timing and specificity of feedback, the level of informational and emotional support. We can even say how different individuals in various jobs may react differently. But how easily does that stretch to the appraisal process?

If HR is based on the scientific understanding of workers, three questions follow: Whence all the differences between different companies? Why is the HR function loathed and despised by so many, including managers? And why do so many initiatives not work? Back to the lab then.

N. 'SCONCEABLE' OFFENCES

What is the first record of political correctness (PC)? The PC virus certainly has infested our world. For some it is simply a mechanism to ensure politeness and prevent numerous other, often subtle manifestations of prejudice, hatefulness or simple rudeness.

For others it is a powerful mind-control mechanism designed to reduce authentic communication, censor beliefs, and stifle humour. Paradoxically, it discourages honesty, making all communication disingenuous, guarded and coded.

Certainly, the old idea that 'sticks and stones may break my bones, but words can never harm me' has long been dispensed with. It appeared that if you follow the law, words are among the most powerful interpersonal weapons of all time.

A broken leg heals; it is only one part of the body that experiences the problem; visible wounds can elicit pity and help. But the broken spirit – the shredded ego, the deflated self-concept – may take years even to partly recover. Drugs, therapists, self-help regimes may be prolonged and cost a great deal.

Some people recall a petty slight from decades before. The off-hand remark from a caustic teacher, the deliberate insult from a playground bully, the deeply hurtful comment from a first girl/boyfriend as the relationship ended. Healed physical illnesses are soon forgotten. That is not the case with nasty – if true – words.

You can try to legislate what goes on in the playground. Impose as many school rules as you like, but the spirit and behaviour of *Lord of the Flies* returns. Maybe 't was ever thus? Perhaps it has a Darwinian survival usefulness. Did resilient, hardy adults, able to cope well with the slings and arrows of misfortune, learn their adaptability when confronted with all those typical childhood experiences?

Adults, on the other hand, may be, or should be, better at understanding how to refrain from insulting, hurting or abusing their colleagues. Some topics are best avoided to ensure more harmonious interactions. And etiquette procedures have been devised precisely for this purpose.

In some Oxbridge colleges, the rules are whispered to newcomers. First, there is the Boston switch: talk to the person to the left during the first course, the right during the second course, left again for the third, etc. This ensures that, however dull, dreary or introverted your fellow diners are, they will not be ignored. Second, only talk about subjects of general and topical interest. Do not show off and talk about your discipline. A classicist, a chemist and a cartographer should be able to find, explore and enjoy a conversation around some issue that amuses them all. Third, the 'sconceable' offence: no talk of politics, religion or women. Yes, women – those were the days of single sex colleges dominated by men. These three topics were out of bounds because they tapped into issues that could generate too much emotion. The quiet, hyper-rational logician could, it was feared, become a barking mad fascist or communist, given licence to talk about how we should be governed. And no talk either about the arts, history, the natural world or travel. Sport can work well for those interested in it, of course.

The punishment for rule breaking was to drink a large beaker ('sconce') of some alcoholic substance (beer, wine, etc.). To the undergraduate this might seem a real incentive to breaking the rules, but to the greying don it was a disgrace, perhaps being rendered speechless or incoherent after the imbibition.

The problem, of course, is that so many simple topics can soon trigger a political discussion. The state of the economy, global warming, even holidays can soon lead to a polarization of so called deniers and embracers, left- vs right-wing opinions. But old hands at this gentle art learn to steer the conversation away from the really hot issues.

The Oxbridge High Table approach seems quaintly ridiculous to the modern politically correct manager, perhaps indoctrinated by a 'diversity at work' course, or having been badly burnt at a tribunal concerning an insulted worker out for a large compensation package.

So what are the rules at work? Could/should/can we legislate for how people behave in their lunch break? Could we have sconceable offences in the canteen, where the cost of breaking the rules is to give time or money to charity, rather than swallow a bellyful of booze?

What about pinning up one of those notices found in public swimming pools, with a long list of 'don'ts' and 'no's': no diving, running, drinking, pushing, shouting. By the time you have read the instruction kit, it seems there is almost nothing you are allowed to do except snooze (no snoring) in a prescribed space (no marking of territory) for a few minutes.

The problem with rule making is the unintended consequences. Make it too difficult to shoot the breeze with colleagues and staff will eat at their desks, forcing the canteen to close, seriously lowering morale and increasing absenteeism.

It is difficult to prevent people seeking out like-minded others who share their values. So there can be dramatic demographic divisions at work. People of similar age, gender, religion and experience prefer to sit, eat and natter together. This may be just what you want because they are less likely to insult one another easily.

Others don't like this self-imposed apartheid and try to facilitate better integration. Various subtle forms of socio-technical manipulations are put in place to force interaction of radically different groups. This can work well in the long term, and helps people discover what they really share in common. But it can lead to fireworks. These can vary from complaints about awful smells emanating from the microwave room to dispensations for religions observation.

O. SHAPERS OF DESTINY

All successful leaders provide much the same narrative of the factors that influenced them most. Studies across organizations in different sectors as well as those within big corporations and across different corporate and national cultures – even different historical time zones – reveal the same story. This is now so clear that academics, somewhat uncharacteristically, call for no further work to be done in this area.

Again and again they mention six powerful learning experiences. Be they famous for start-ups or turna-rounds, be they great captains of industry or mega-rich entrepreneurs, or be they well known or respected leaders in government, education or the military, the same six factors were mentioned.

As previously discussed in Part I, the first is *early work experience*. This maybe a 'part-time' Saturday job at school; a relatively unskilled summer holiday job at university; or one of the first jobs they ever had. For some it was the unadulterated tedium or monotony they felt powerfully motivated never to be condemned to. For others it was a particular work style or process that they have retained all their lives.

Many people have 'false starts','try-outs' or 'first goes' to see where their passions and interests match their ability and talents. For many, work comes as a bit of a shock: following the strict time schedules, the witnessing of widespread pilfering, known management distrust and dislikes. Its memory sticks at an impressive age.

The second factor is the *experience of other people* and is nearly always an immediate boss, but it could be a colleague or one of the serious grown-ups. They are almost always remembered as either very bad or very good: both teach lessons. What always or never to do. Just as we parent as we were parented, so many manage as they were managed. Unless, of course, one had a model that suggested otherwise.

Some people vow never to repeat the negative, humiliating control-freakishness of an early boss. Others remember and try to copy the guide, mentor and supervisor who taught them so much. It's a bit like the inspirational teacher who changed one for life, who gave one confidence, excited the imagination and made work fun. Or, of course, the one who in a few weeks succeeded in putting one off cricket or chemistry forever.

The third factor was *short-term assignments*: project work, standing in for another or interim management. Because this takes people out of their comfort zone and exposes them to issues and problems they never before confronted they learn quickly. For some it is the lucky break: serendipity provides an opportunity to find a new skill or passion.

Fourth, but for many top of their list, the *first major life assignment*. This is often the first promotion, foreign posting or departmental move to a higher position. It is often recalled because suddenly the stakes were higher, everything more complex and novel and ambiguous. There were more pressures and the buck stopped with one. You were accountable. Suddenly the difficulties of management became real.

The fifth factor can be subsumed under the above for many people. It comprises *hardships* of various kinds. It is about attempting to cope in a crisis which may be professional or personal. It teaches one the real value of things: technology, loyal staff and supportive head offices. The experiences are those of battle-hardened soldiers or the 'been there, seen that' brigade.

Hardship teaches many lessons: how resourceful and robust some people can be and how others panic and cave in. It teaches some to admire a fit and happy organization when they see it. It teaches them to distinguish between needs and wants. It teaches a little about minor forms of post-traumatic stress disorder. And the virtues of stoicism, hardiness and a tough mental attitude.

However down on the list come in-house training programmes. Some remember and quote their *MBA experience*; far fewer some specific (albeit fiendishly expensive) course. One or two quote the experience of receiving *360-degree feedback*. More recall a *coach*, though it could be because they were so good or so awful.

Rather bad news for trainers, business school teachers and coaches. Here is the bottom line from this research … and the implications of it. First, work experience, like early stretch assignments, is the best way to teach leadership. Inevitably some experiences are better than others because they teach different lessons in different ways. And some people seem to acquire these valuable experiences despite, rather than a result of, company policy.

Experiential learning takes time but timing is important. It's not a steady, orderly accumulation of insights and skills. Some experiences teach little or indeed bad habits.

But three factors conspire to defeat the experimented model. First, both young managers and their bosses want to short circuit it: do it faster, cheaper, better. Hence the appeal of the one-minute manager, the one-day MBA and the short course. Second many HR professionals see this approach as dis-experiencing them because they are 'in charge' of the leadership development programme. Third, some of those see experience as a list, not a developmental exercise.

So two findings. First, maybe leadership potential and talent should be defined as the ability to learn from experience. Second, every move, promotion or challenge should be assessed also from its learning potential. The best development plan or learning strategy for any executives is to define what people need to learn to do; what experiences offer the best opportunities to learn them; how through feedback, support even incentives to ensure the latter; and of course find the people eager and able to learn from experience.

P. THE TALENT MYTH

It had to come. Pride before the fall. Wasteful management fad. Pointless expenditure. Talent is a myth. Talent management is bogus nonsense.

The nature–nurture pendulum has the property of swinging wildly one way or the other. In the 1960s genetics and biology were out. Everything was environmentally determined. Then we understood DNA, the socio-biologists emerged and everything was determined by our genes, our caveman past and simple processes of adaptation.

But the pendulum has (inevitably) swung back. And this time the 'culprit' is sports 'science'. It is sometimes called the *10,000 hours rule*. And it states that, whatever your ability, build or aptitude, you (or anybody else) can show expert talented performance with (as little as) 10,000 hours of coached, motivated and structured practice. The magic ingredient is the *power law of practice*: the speed of completing a task well is a function of the number of task trials.

Practice not only makes perfect. It makes talent. So if you practise yet you don't succeed in winning an Olympic Gold, appearing at the Albert/Carnegie Hall or starting a hugely successful company, it is *not* that you simply don't have the talent, but rather that you have not practised enough or have not done it right.

It's the old line of 'everyone has talent'. You make your talent . . . no matter the cards you have been dealt. No matter the fact you may not have chosen your parents well. Little importance those first seven years as the Jesuits would have you believe. You can do it.

It seems common sense goes straight out of the window when guru – greedy management, writers or motivational speakers – try to interpret the science for their own ends.

It seems quite reasonable to assert that practice is an essential component to elite, expert or excellent performance, be it on the sports field, in the examination hall or in the office. Necessary, but hardly sufficient. Get a good coach, work hard, have a good practice schedule. But is that enough for real success?

However much focused, deliberate practice is undertaken, it is always constrained or limited. Start with physique. Look at sprinters, swimmers, pole-vaulters. Notice not only their practice-induced musculature, but their height, leg length, foot size. They are remarkably similar for each sport and often somewhat different from the normal population.

And what about age? How many 50-year-old sprinters do you notice? Things wear out, become weaker, don't function as well. Even early experience is crucial. The earlier you start playing the violin, skiing, speaking German, the easier it is to be proficient and – with practice – expert.

But here's the rub. The sheer amount of practice cannot finally explain the very real and manifestly apparent differences between elite or expert performers. Take 10 people, put them through the same well-designed but gruelling 15–20,000-hour practice programme, and one is a star, another an also-ran. That is latent talent.

Talent is not innate or fixed. It is potential that needs shaping. The seed is important but so is the soil, the fertilizer and the nutrients.

Some people learn faster than others. The skill comes more easily and quickly. They are naturals. They take to practice. Even when putting in maximum practice some people are constrained by natural limitations in physiology, morphology (shape) or capacity (intellect).

The investment theorists argue that talent comes from the application of motivation to ability. So people have different learning experiences and they exhibit their opportunities in quite different ways. The bright, curious child reads more and therefore becomes more knowledgeable.

Through experience people find out more about their likes and more about their abilities. Some experience early failure, which then becomes self-fulfilling. The belief they have little skill or talent in an area means they avoid it, practise little and never master it. Others persist, possibly driven by inner competitiveness or pushy parents. They are deeply appetitive. Driven to being successful. Willing to put in effort. Okay about dealing with setbacks.

Some are driven by others. Take out the parent, the teacher or the coach and their motivation to practise dwindles. It's the opposite of 'falling among thieves'. Stay in the right crowd and the motivation to succeed develops. Take them away and the idea of the 10,000 hours to ensure success becomes deeply demotivating.

Different skills place different demands on an individual's assets. These are necessary but not sufficient to become talented. People differ enormously in their passions and capacity to invest in their talents. Outside influences can help people over their performance plateaus by only so much.

So talent is not a genetic endowment. It is not something that only needs to be 'discovered' within. But neither is it something you can acquire by will power alone. Talent for sport, for business, for art means in part having the right base requirements. Size and shape of body and brain. But it also requires hard work. Perspiration and inspiration. It is sad, but true, that not everyone has talent. Yes Britain has *some* talent. Desire to be talented is not enough. Hard work, indeed 100,000 hours of practice, will not suffice.

You get into the talent group by effort and ability. The less ability, the more effort is required. But there are minimum requirements for both.

The Daily Grind

It is tough at the top, and tough all the way up. Things go wrong. There are bad apples in every barrel. People inside and outside the organization let you down. There are sudden changes in the economy and in the law. And that is where resilience is really tested.

We have increasingly to work with people who are not like us. People from a different culture or age group or gender. We have to get used to new working arrangements. Moreover, the resilient leader has to be ahead of the game and help to bring about that change, not just follow the trend.

Management can be remorseless. The daily grind can weaken people to the point that they seriously underperform. The resilient manager can deal with the stresses and setbacks better than his/her less resilient colleagues and keep going in the toughest times.

A. A GRIM PLACE TO WORK

For over 10 years the *Sunday Times* has produced an annual list of the '*100 Best Companies to Work For*'. Alongside the list are examples of policies and practices that survey-based data have shown to lead to employee satisfaction.

The methodology looks at various broad topics/issues: First, perceptions of the type and quality of *leadership* employees experience. Second, their personal levels of *well-being*, stress and health at work. Third, their attitudes to, beliefs about, and experience of their *immediate boss*/manager/supervisor. Fourth, how they feel about *their team*, their colleagues and their immediate peers. Fifth, their attitude to *the deal* or, more prosaically, to their pay and conditions, benefits and remuneration. Sixth, *payback* to the local community and society in general: to what extent the company is a good corporate citizen. Seventh, general feelings towards the *employing organization*. Eighth, *personal growth*, or the extent to which they feel challenged by their job, helping them to upgrade and use their skills base.

Inevitably, the public sector does better at some things (fair deal, payback) than others (leadership, well-being). Small companies seem to do better than big ones. Flat organizations do better than tall. And many pay serious attention to the exercise, believing that it can lead to seriously good PR and indeed may attract a better quality of employee in the future.

But what about data or attitudes to absenteeism, bullying, CEOs' outrageous salaries, harassment, nepotism or union involvement? How about a name and shame *worst* companies to work for? Would this be little more than a licence for angry, alienated, failing employees to criticize their organization anonymously. Every organization has its share of disillusioned, passive-aggressive resisters. They are blockers of change, heart-sinking colleagues, super-snipers of supervisors.

They won't go when offered good voluntary retirement packages and they sour and poison the workplace for others, particularly new recruits. Frequently, their negativity has developed over time, for these people are often the products of poorly managed companies, lazy or incompetent managers. They did not start off their journey this way. Certainly, they would not have been hired had any of this negativity been detected. But they became disaffected after what happened to them and others around them.

It is clearly not only the '*nyet* mindset', sour employees who believe they work for the worst company in the area/country/sector. Even the most sanguine, stable and forgiving employees can find themselves working for a terrible company.

So what are the criteria? Certainly it is not just *the absence* of the qualities that make a company great to work for. Just as we know that different factors cause happiness as opposed to unhappiness, so it is clear that there would be very different factors involved in creating the '100 Worst Companies to Work For'.

Perhaps the first criterion would be *widespread hypocrisy*. This means where the reality of working there and the vision/mission/values/propaganda are poles apart. This is a gap analysis where the actual beliefs and behaviours of the top people reflect the very opposite of all those pious corporate values they espouse. Call it 'expression aspirational values', 'impression management' or simply 'lies'.

Second, there is *stifling bureaucracy*. These are companies which have rules and procedures for everything – from what is available in the canteen to how you present yourself on Facebook. They are, it seems, terrified of idiosyncratic creativity, of people expressing their individuality. Like totalitarian states, they pre- and proscribe all aspects of your life. A *Nineteen Eighty-Four* world of automatons marching in time to the beat of management drums.

Third, there is *heavily disguised favouritism*. This encompasses all the real issues of discrimination, nepotism and in-group bias. In effect, mobility and success have little to do with effort and ability, but rather with being a member of a group – be that Oxbridge graduates, pale males, or those with a particular belief system. Or worse, the in-group are those sharing a particular style or philosophy. An example may be attitudes to employee motivation: keep them cold and keep them hungry, sticks work better than carrots, big lies are best. Very different – all significant for the workplace.

Fourth, a *win-lose* (vs win-win) philosophy. This applies as much inside the company as the way it sees the opposition. It sacrifices all aspects of co-operation for competition. You fight for space, for tools, for rewards. If I have them, you can't. The philosophy is bitterly Darwinian.

Fifth, *chronic instability*. This is not a reaction to an unstable world, but the result of frantic and persistent chopping and changing as one restructuring, rebranding, relocation follows another with very little by way of a long-term plan. Nothing like change mania to cause capsizing.

Finally, *erratic management*, which sums up everything. Those in supervisor or management roles are undertrained and overpaid; they are all head and no heart. They set impossible targets but give little support. The only time you see your supervisor is when you get a bollocking; the only time you see the CEO is on the news apologizing or trying to worm his way out of the latest crisis.

Anyone want to score their company on the above six and start the alternative 100 companies list?

B. AESTHETICS AT WORK

What values do the art and architecture of organizations communicate? How much PR and advertising value do you get from your organizational exteriors and interiors? You can communicate state-of-the-art, cutting-edge science, an eye for classical beauty, and orderly, conservative solemnity or pragmatic utilitarianism. And even if the outside is dull, drab and dreamy you certainly do something about the inside. While some buildings have old and iconic value (the Hoover Building, the Lloyds Building, the 'Gherkin'), some organizations seem quite happy to work in dull, functional buildings.

Visit Tesco's vs Sainsbury's headquarters and you experience some contrast. The former is tucked away down a side street of an obscure village (Cheshunt) 30 minutes from London, while the latter makes a statement of glass in Holborn, yards away from the city of London.

Buildings make statements about those who inhabit them. And, if you are an environmental determinist, they affect the very behaviour in them. Consider how the House of Commons perpetuates the two-party system or that the British Airways Waterside building keeps people in it.

Some banks do conspicuous consumption: large empty spaces in places which command some of the highest space rates in the world. Some organizations are so concerned with security, the first thing that greets you are barriers and bouncer-like characters standing in macho positions, dressed in ill-fitting suits.

There is an academic literature on aesthetic preference: preference for art and music, film and poetry, architecture and dance. Each area has its genres which act as a convenient category scheme for researchers. So you can ask (at least the aesthetically literate) whether they prefer cubism or surrealism or fascism over romanticism in art, what they think about art deco buildings or their taste in jazz.

Some art forms are taken seriously by organizations. Try to notice the effect of music at work. Shops use music to change mood and pace, and so do restaurants. Music is played while you are 'on hold'. Restaurants play music for 'effect'. We still have music while you work in those almost disappeared, dull manufacturing jobs.

But what music? Fast or slow? Modern or classical? Vocal or instrumental? Minor or major key? For some, like buskers, their livelihood is determined by it. Quiz them and see if 'their takings' are affected by time-of-day musical interactions. That is, does the same music played at different times of the day have a radically different effect on the coins thrown into the hat? Should one play different music at up-market tube stations (e.g.

Hampstead)? Is the saxophone more profit-yielding than the guitar?

But what about the visual arts? You are about to commission a design for a new headquarters building, perhaps in a big city or on more land outside the town. You expect lots of important people to visit your building. It may even feature in a new logo or in the icons on your letter headed paper. You want it to communicate your values. How do you brief the architect?

And once built, how do you decorate it inside? How do you best use the space to communicate what you believe it can stand for?

C. BISCUIT HUNTERS, FILM EXTRAS, THERAPY PATIENTS

It has been known for a long time that volunteers are quite different from conscripts. From a military perspective it was thought one of the former was worth, infighting skill, determination and mentality, 10 of the latter. Indeed, this was demonstrated in the Falklands War.

Psychologists have shown that volunteers are different from non-volunteers in a host of personality, values and ability factors. In fact, the results of many studies are threatened by this methodological error – that is, people who volunteer to participate in research studies are statistically unrepresentative of the general population.

This is a serious issue for pollsters, social scientists and all those involved in market research. How to get a good, honest, representative sample? A normal sample from which one could derive population norms. The first approach is to try incentives. These only partially work because those with less money and more time on their hands tend to respond. The problem is you can't easily get at those who are beyond small incentives. Ask a marketing person how they reach Social Class 1, middle-aged men. Not many people with clipboards wait outside the opera or polo matches.

The problem of reaching representative volunteers is a problem even for the justice system. Take jury service. The terror of serving on a jury is to be holed up for days with a representative sample of 12 people. But are they? Who has escaped? The astute, the sly and the rich manage to escape even legal injunctions.

There are other rewards that people have identified as possible incentives for taking part in a focus group, mini-survey or an interview on the street. Indeed, there are known categories of people who respond to different types of reward.

The first are sometimes called '*biscuit hunters*'. They are a little bit like 'compers', obsessive competition entrants. They seek out focus groups. After all, a focus group is like going to a party where you are fed and watered . . . and paid. Some groups restrict volunteers by demography. You might have to be over 45, or a young mother, or live in the Midlands.

But more often, you only have to express an interest in some product or service and you are welcome. An ideal setting for the bored housewife, the hungry postgraduate, or the writer with a block. A nice room, lots of refreshments, some potentially interesting new friends, and the group supervised by a 'strict nanny' who will keep everything running smoothly. A wonderful party atmosphere. And, best of all, people who take your opinions seriously.

Next there are the *film extras*. These are people desperate to appear on television. Some hover in high streets hoping for a spot of *vox pop*. Others are prepared to queue up for days to audition for some programme where they may be little more than people in a crowd.

They come in all shapes and sizes, but they have one thing in common: the naïve belief that (a) they are stars in the waiting (b) they will be, or certainly deserve to

be, discovered (c) their lives will change forever for the
better once they are discovered. Most are wrong on all
counts, but may spend 20 years finding out. It certainly
makes the job of those doing crowd scenes interesting.

The third type of volunteer may be the saddest of all.
They are those wanting *therapy*, sympathy or counselling. Some think that they have a wonderful story to
tell. Others that they are deserving because of 'all they
have been through'. The majority may be self-obsessed.
Terrible bores, they are desperate to find opportunities
where others are prepared to listen to them.

Paradoxically, many believe they would make good
therapists themselves, despite their chronic lack of self-
insight and low self-awareness. Further, because they
seem always to be on 'transmit' and never on 'receive',
they make terrible listeners.

But boy, do they search out opportunities to pour out
their woes on some unsuspecting innocent.

So there we have it: biscuit hunters, film extras and
therapy patients. The psychology of the volunteer who
waits to be heard, seen or helped. Some may advance from
one condition to the other in their attempt to be noticed.

And they are all a problem and a nuisance. They take
up time and energy. Above all, when grouped together,
they form an abnormal, not representative, sample of
the population.

D. CHANGING PLACES

So, the Palace of Westminster needs a bit of repair work.
The usual story: an old building; problems with the wir-
ing, leaking pipes, even asbestos. The tale of the fearless
mouse in the restaurant is delightful. And it is perhaps
preferable that the rats come to Parliament as squeaking
rodents rather than as representatives of the people.

But how to proceed? Move out for a set period and
let the workmen get in to do their stuff? Do it in stages,

moving about the half-closed building trying to carry on as usual with all the noise, mess and space restrictions? Sell the place to make room for a new and glamorous seven-star hotel, like Admiralty Arch? Decamp to Salford or Slough and save the taxpayer some money?

It has been observed that the only man ever to enter Parliament with a coherent policy was Guy Fawkes, but his solution to the problem is probably not that welcome.

Perhaps this refurbishment offers the best opportunity that we have ever seen for radical change in the Mother of Parliaments. It is all about environmental determinism and alteration. Churchill, after the bombing of the House of Commons in 1941, insisted that it be perfectly restored to exactly how it was because, he argued, 'We shape our buildings, and afterwards they shape us.'

The House of Commons is built for two parties: Blue team and Red team. They face each other at a distance that does not inhibit snarling and very polite gestures of disdain. Yellow team seems not to know where to sit. We have an adversarial, two-party system, determined by the very shape of the debating chamber.

There seems to be a persuasive British view that argument and debate facilitate better-decision making. The BBC has taken up this idea with enthusiasm, having lists of strange eccentrics prepared to debate any issue. Thus, if a physicist has the temerity to suggest the world is round, the BBC can find the chairman of the Flat Earth Society to take him on. Actually, it all seems a bit Hegelian, with thesis, antithesis and then synthesis.

The shape of other national debating chambers is different. See the Welsh and Scottish assemblies . . . much more 'theatre in the round'. Much more 'representative democracy'.

The environmental determinists are supported by architects who want to suggest that their buildings can have miraculous effects on aspects of the human psyche, such as morale and productivity. Remember the arguments for open-plan offices so eagerly taken up by managers who realized the massive cost savings of the whole enterprise? Open-plan offices, we were told, encouraged better communication, leading to increased employee satisfaction and therefore higher profits. A happy family atmosphere, so different from the cold indifference of people sitting in their own enclosed offices, communicating only electronically with colleagues.

All of which was evidence-free propaganda, of course. Open-plan offices led to Dilbert-like cubicles where people built higher and higher partitions to give themselves some privacy and communicated less. They hid from each other as much as possible and personalized their reduced spaces with photographs and nick-nacks to establish their territory. What would happen if you banned partitions and *then* measured morale and productivity? Look at how the meeting rooms are used (and abused). Observe the need for privacy and space.

Old reactionary nonsense? We are told that people get used to it, young people like it, extroverts thrive, productivity goes up. And the evidence, please? For some jobs, perhaps. For most, not.

But anyone who has had an office move knows how very powerful the experience is. The predominant reason is that it changes relationships at work that are formed and maintained by propinquity (proximity). We get to know, like and talk to those on the same floor. This is partly why we get the dreaded silos: people doing the same job need to interact a lot, so you put them in the same office where they develop a unique culture . . . and possibly a suspicion and even dislike of people from other parts of the organization on different sites.

Silos are bad, so it is said. They reduce co-operation and increase competition: they reduce trust and increase suspicion. What we need is matrix management . . . or some such idea. But the real reason why silos develop is that people with similar interests, values and abilities are attracted to certain jobs and are therefore like each other. And those who are like each other, like each other and find co-operation easy.

Moving offices changes interaction patterns. It also alienates the established and the powerful who have over the years shrewdly found the best locations: the biggest, quietest, most out-of-the-way. The corner office, the room with a view.

And moves have the habit of giving people either equal space or quirky options where there are apparently many trade-offs. This can seriously disrupt all those subtle signals of power and prestige.

A wise change-agent CEO, whose job it was to resuscitate a seriously failing organization, started to 'unfreeze' the set ways by demanding that everyone move office, but remain on the same sight. It seemed random and it very nearly was. But it had the huge benefit of both signalling what was to come and what it meant.

A wonderful opportunity, then, to reform the Commons . . . and the Lords next.

E. GENDER AT WORK

First there was the glass ceiling, then the glass escalator, next the glass cliff. Glass doors and floors followed. The terms are usually but not exclusively used to describe the handicaps that women face in senior management advancement. These barriers are real but invisible. Women don't know about them until they bump into them: it hurts the body and the soul . . . and the sense of justice in the world.

The feeling is that, despite rhetoric to the contrary, various forms of (upward) mobility are not available to certain groups. The glass ceiling prevents further promotion, the glass escalator promises that which it does not and cannot deliver. The glass cliff is there as a trap to 'force' certain groups to fail. Glass doors are real, yet unseen, blocks, etc.

The idea that certain groups can't make it to the top is, of course, not restricted to women. Minority groups – be they racial, religious or linguistic – have made the claim. There is a long list of 'isms', such as the new 'shapism' and 'bodyism', that suggests people make assumptions and thence decisions on a person's body mass index and overall shape. Skinny and tubby people don't make it.

The literature on gender at work has seen two sides take up mutually viciously hostile positions. The evolutionary psychologists supported by the sociobiologists, take a Venus women, Mars men perspective. There are differences; they are hardwired; they have consequences; live with it!

Opposed to them is an array of people, from angry feminists to anthropo-culturo- environmento-socio types who think (nearly) all human characteristics are the products of society. They argue then that any sex differences at work result from some sort of discrimination and need to be 'redefined' immediately by strict legal changes; punishment of discriminators of all types, and monitoring of all organizations.

The sociobiology books sell well. They offer wonderful 'explanations' for common observations. Why do men favour blondes? And blue-eyed blondes at that? Why do older women rarely have long hair? They celebrate simple one-liners, such as 'boys like things, girls like people', 'boys compete, girls co-operate', or even 'women value relationships, men value work'.

Some publish data showing that most maths, physics and chemistry teachers are men. Or that in some jobs, such as air traffic controller, nuclear engineer, racing car driver, over 90 per cent of the job holders are men. The hardwired sex-difference people point out all the data that show sex differences in infancy, preschool and high school. They note that the male brain *systematizes* and is designed for tool making, weapon use, etc., while the female brain *empathizes*. This is designed for mothering, making friends and allies.

They note that boys express more self-competence in sport and maths, and girls in reading and music.

The biological boffins point out that sex differences are observed across time, cultures and species because they are the basis of evolutionary specialization. These sex differences are brain differences: hardwired. They argue that sex-typed activities appear before gender aware-ness. And now they have sexy new toys that demonstrate these inherent differences. Undeniable, empirically based science.

The other team rejects all this as a mix of bogus sci-ence or simply proof of discrimination. Why are all the authors men? Is there not in what they say a heady mix-ture of the most awful 'isms' like racism and the long, dark shadow of eugenics.

It does seem clear, however, that the world of most business organizations favours males, who are vastly over-represented in leadership positions. The elaborate hierarchies and power- distance structures feed male sta-tus aspirations. Men run the show: government, business, the lot. They always have and they always will . . . and, say the socio-biologists, there is good reason for it. Pointless having all this legislation capping the percentages of males.

The social learning theorists argue that the constant stress on competitiveness is the male way of doing things. Further, all the talk of goals, targets and strategies is designed to satisfy male achievement motivation. Also, work tasks are made specialized to fit the non-multi-tasking, single-minded focus that is found in males.

Some organizations are more masculine than others. The more masculine the culture, the more male val-ues, such as advancement, earning, freedom and prob-lem solving, are emphasized. That is what males prefer.

The data suggest feminine cultures pay more attention to the social aspects of the job, to a friendly, congenial atmosphere, to the physical working conditions and to the ease of work. So it is people vs things, quality of life vs quantity of life, work to live vs live to work, service ideal vs achievement ideal, interdependence vs independence. And masculine types are attracted to masculine industries and vice versa. So be it.

Whichever side of the fence one prefers to sit, one experiential fact is clear. Any workplace that is exclusively male or female is made much better psychologically by having a few members of the opposite sex. Leaders and managers will point out that boardroom behaviour is much more normal and productive if a few women temper the testosterone-fuelled duels of the adversarial males.

F. GENERATIONS AT WORK 1

Some call them generations, others cohorts. And each has its own label, be it 'Traditionalists'/'Old Fogeys'; 'Baby Boomers'/ 'The Spoilt-Sixties Generation'. Then there is 'Generation X' – that often lamented lost generation, and the hopeful 'Millennials'.

Generations are distinguishable most by their attitudes and values, shaped by their personal experiences. Growing up at a particular time and place often leaves a very strong mark on individuals. After all, societies try to socialize people into a set of beliefs and values about all the big issues: right/wrong, good/bad, just/unjust, fair/unfair.

Most people within a cohort supposedly fail to see the power of the forces on them that shape their views. They see only differences and variability between themselves and are often unaware of the similarities. Paradoxically, they see other generations as 'all the same' and often treat them with suspicion, while noticing how varied their own generation is. In psychobabble this is called 'out group homogeneity' and 'in group heterogeneity'.

Inevitably, generational differences play out in the workplace.

Traditionalists are, it is said, products of the safe and secure 1950s. They were and are cautious, conformist, conservative. They prefer structure and security. They understand loyalty and the concept of a career. They weren't and aren't very mobile and therefore have little experience of any type of diversity. They knew and accepted class divisions inside and outside work and experienced relatively little technological change. Most are now quietly retired doing the garden and falling off the perch at a significant rate.

The Baby Boomers were shaped by the turbulent 1960s, when they challenged the assumptions and what they saw to be the complacency of their elders. This was the generation of civil rights, Woodstock, moon landings, sit-ins, hijackings and nuclear power. Think Hippies and Flower Power, but also Vietnam and race riots.

The Baby Boomers were anti-conformist and anti-hierarchical. They did not like uniforms or uniformity. They were happy to experiment. After all, sexual intercourse began in 1963. And many enjoyed shocking others. They were rebels with a cause. And they were often disruptive at work. They distrusted authority and like change for change's sake.

Some have refused to age gracefully and enjoy shocking their children with their outrageous behaviour. The 'alternative' family in the various 'Fockers' films nicely sums up the type.

Generation X-ers were shaped by the turbulent times of the 1970s and 1980s. They experienced the worst depression since the 1930s. They saw the rise of the women's movement, the green lobby and the end of manufacturing industry in the UK. They also witnessed the massive advance in computer technology and use.

More importantly, they saw mass unemployment and compulsory redundancy. They saw the last gasp of the old trades unions, militant Thatcherism and the Winter of Discontent. It was not a pretty picture.

Generation X-ers often got a bad press at work. They were neither conformist, nor anti-conformist. If anything, they tended to be alienated. They felt little loyalty to those who showed little loyalty to them. They were the 'me' not the 'we' generation and were told 'greed is good'. They saw the world at work as a jungle and survival of the fittest as the name of the game.

Millennials joined the world of work around the year 2000. They had been shaped by the 1990s: the end of the USSR, the unification of Germany, the end of apartheid. And most of all, globalization. Technology shrank the world and therefore profoundly affected it.

Businesses chased the cheapest labour force, whether through increasing numbers of legal or illegal migrants or simply relocating factories and call centres to different parts of the world. Diversity at work wasn't an option; it was a reality and a necessity.

And machines replaced people. People became nomads – they hot-bunked without offices, working out of their cars, hotel rooms and sheds in the bottom of their gardens. Email replaced snail mail, cameras recorded one's comings and goings, and pensions were threatened.

Thus, we are told we have to be very sensitive to generational differences and how to manage them. It may seem at first reading that people from different generations are from different planets, quite unable to understand and appreciate each other. Baby Boomers are from Mars, Millennials from Venus.

Different generations have very different expectations of the world of work. That is the message, but it is simple-minded, guru-led tosh. It is based on the assumption that attitudes to, and behaviour at, work are powerfully shaped by early socialization. That socioeconomic and political events that shaped one's early life left such an impression as to make us all carriers of a time capsule.

This is wrong on three counts. First, it ignores the simple act of ageing. People do change over time to some extent and so the Millennials may end up just like the Baby Boomers at the same age and stage. Second, it assumes that social experience is more powerful than ability, personality and values in shaping work attitudes and behaviours. Put a dozen people of similar age in the room and see how different they are as a function of their education, social class and personality. Third, make arbitrary cut-off points for categorization just as historians used to classify the reigns of monarchs. So, if you're born a few years either side of a date, you change category.

There are plenty of popular books on 'the generations'. And they make amusing reading, but it is just another fad that will soon disappear to Oxfam bookshops. There is more to understanding employees' attitudes at work than the date they were born.

G. GENERATIONS AT WORK 2

Given they had much the same ability, experience and skills, how likely would you be to hire a Generation X-er or a Millennial or a Baby Boomer over a Veteran? Think of a relatively simple job such as a waiter or shop assistant. Or perhaps someone who works in a call centre or on a help desk.

There is now quite clearly a *Generation at Work* industry. Media articles, TV shows, books and seminars, practitioners and consultants are now all *generationists*. Everything can be explained by date of birth. We are victims of our cohort, shaped by the forces of our time. Forget personality and ability, genetics and biology. It was the war, or the hippies, or the 9/11 attitudes that shaped us. Somehow it was the ideology and worldwide events of our formative years that had such a long-term impact.

The 'theory' goes that major (national and international) cultural, historical and social events have a direct impact on a person's attitudes, beliefs and values. So, whether you grew up in rural Argentina, urban Austria or suburban Australia at the same time (historic period), you have a lot in common. Tosh – where are the data to support this nonsense? The plural of anecdote is, alas, not evidence.

So, the generationists tell us, we have materialistic and time-stressed Baby Boomers, individualistic and sceptical Generation X-ers, narcissistic, cynical but socially conscious Millennials. Such a Western and narrow perspective.

There are, of course, doubts about how you define these different generations, what you call them and precisely how many are there in the workforce. The Veterans (or Traditionalists) have around 1925–1945 as their birth dates, the Baby Boomers around 1945–1965, Generation X and Y 1965–1985 and the Millennials any time after 1985. Roughly – very roughly. And then there is the arbitrariness of the dates, which means two siblings born a year apart come from different groups.

So how many are there now in the workforce? About 5–10 per cent are Traditionalists; 30–40 per cent Baby Boomers; 30 per cent Generation X-ers; the remainder (20–30 per cent) Millennials.

The gurus tell us with more self-confidence than evidence that there are all sorts of differences between these various groups.

Popularists describe clear differences between the generations which, they tell employers they should take into consideration regarding recruitment, selection, training, compensation and benefits, promotion and even termination. Some are tech-phobic, others techno-philic. Some have the work ethic in abundance; others seem to have almost nothing.

The academics have, however, been beavering away trying to see if there are really generational differences in work-related behaviour. Just recently (2012) a group at George Washington University published a meta-analysis in the *Journal of Business and Psychology*. They looked at 20 studies covering many jobs. These studies tended to look at aspects like generational differences in job satisfaction, commitment and intention to leave.

The results were predictable but somewhat disappointing. They showed that the older generation were happier, more committed and less likely to leave their jobs. But the differences were small and the results of different studies not altogether similar enough to give a general picture.

The problem with this research is threefold. The first is to do with cross-sectional vs longitudinal research (i.e. you take snapshots at one particular moment rather than follow people through time). It is never clear if the results are an effect of aging or generation. Indeed it may be quite easy to explain all the findings by the age factor alone. Older people are often better paid and more secure, accounting for all the findings.

It could be that as people become more socially confident, less anxious, and more conscientious over time – irrespective of their generation – they become more satisfied with their lives *and* their jobs. Further, as people mature and (they hope) progress upwards, their (better) jobs are characterized by greater autonomy and skill variety and seem more significant – all of which predict job satisfaction.

So where have we got to with the generation idea? Not too far. No real theory as to how it works, and little real data to support the claims. All hype, no evidence. Yet another guru and journalist-inspired fad? Partly.

What determines work outcomes such as productivity and satisfaction? Certainly, ability and personality play a part. But so do cultural issues. The Poles have done extremely well in Britain as a result of their training and their work ethic. Indian migrants do well because of their stress on education and their family support systems. National and religious culture does play a role and both are shaped by historical events.

So back to the first question: who should you employ? The first factor must be job attitude and aptitude. You can probably correctly assume that younger people compared to older people would be more social-media savvy and computer literate, fitter and stronger, quicker and more agile. But that is an age factor rather than a cohort factor. And there is probably just too much difference between people within any generation to pay much attention to some pretty arbitrary birth date ranges and categorical descriptors.

H. GRIEVANCES AT WORK

Employees all over the Western world are increasingly filing grievance complaints and law suits. Employment tribunals have trebled, even quadrupled, over the past 20–30 years. There is litigation exposure. Aggravated employees are ever more protesting and seeking redress for an incident that has occurred at work.

The academics have caught up with this literature with a timely review by two management theorists (Bernard Walker & Robert Hamilton) in a recent issue of the *International Journal of Management Reviews Vol. 13* (2011).

What is causing this trend? Is work becoming nastier, more dirty and dangerous with bullying b*****ds as supervisors? Or is it because employees now have different expectations at work? What has been the impact of the decline of trades unions and their collective bargaining approach to conflict? And whence the role of avaricious lawyers? Should we blame or thank Judge Judy for the way she deals with these matters? The deregulated

world is different from the old, low technology, manufacturing workplace of our parents. Flat structures, team-
based knowledge workers . . . well, at least for some.

So, first the data. What do we know about the incidence of grievance events? It's difficult to get the stats
for various reasons. There is a great difference between
potential grievances and grievances filed. There are those
reported by mouth and those reported in writing. There
are those dealt with happily, quickly and informally as
opposed to those written grievances that go through the
full process.

The data we have suggest there are many factors that
influence whether the grievance is filed. It's higher in
America (5 per 1000 employees) than Britain (2 per 1000).
It's higher (about twice the rate) in heavily unionized
organizations than in those that are not unionized. It's
higher at bargaining/contract renegotiation time. And it
is clearly more common in some sectors than others.

But, like suicide statistics, grievance figures are difficult to obtain, often fudged and frequently massaged.
Yet we do know the cost is high to the many individuals
concerned: time taken, legal fees, reputations damaged.

Faced with a grievance at work a person can choose to
be a filer (someone who will exercise their voice) or a non-
filer (someone who will say nothing, or quietly leave).

The American data show that filers from union settings tend to be younger, male, better educated and more
skilled than non-filers. Non-union filers also tend to be
young and male but less skilled and educated. In Britain,
they tend to be middle-aged white males in managerial
jobs. So does an employee need testosterone and a bit of
nous to go in for grievance filing?

And then there are the grievance issues. Two big issues
feature in grievances: first, the nature of supervision/
management; and second, job conditions. You guessed
it – nasty, abusive, bullying, demanding, unfair bosses
and unpleasant working conditions with unreasonable

schedules, poor equipment and the presence of electronic monitoring.

So what do the filers want? Restorative justice? Are they mainly motivated by a sense of chronic and acute unfairness and mistreatment or is their real motive economic and political gain? It's a bit like whistle blowing. Do some filers expend huge effort in looking for all minor and trivial signs of unfairness with an eye to humiliating individuals and companies, or getting a nice little 'no-win, no-fee' payment?

Of course, many grievance filers will have to consider the relative utility or attractiveness of filing in the first place. What is the reward–cost ratio for winning? As opposed to saying nothing but seeking perhaps easier revenge through higher absenteeism and counterproductive work behaviours mixed with lower output. Poisoning co-workers' attitudes and mentally moving them into the departure lounge of the organization.

It can be a long process with many stages: discussions with the parties involved, submitting a written grievance, a committee to investigate, third-party arbitration. A central question for the grievance filer is his/her perception that the whole process is accessible, credible and safe. Also that it is understandable, quick and fair. Maybe that is why people like Judge Judy: it's all over in a few minutes, she seems impartial, attentive and well informed, and her judgment is quite final.

All grievance procedures have winners and losers in the formal process. There are short- and long-term benefits. It seems from the data that, overall, most grievances are resolved in the employee's favour. Also, smaller firms are more likely to be involved and more likely to lose, compared to bigger organizations. But, of course, there is a lot of variation.

The major issue surrounds the post-settlement outcome. Imagine the situation: Bolshy Blimp takes his supervisor, Bully-Boy Bloggs, to the tribunal and wins costs and compensation. Then he comes back to work. Perhaps there's a hint of a temptation for Bloggs to retaliate, such that Blimp might have won the grievance battle but has really lost the career war.

This may relate to one fundamental concern: was it a *personal* grievance (i.e. filed about a particular person for his/her behaviour) or a *policy* grievance about some management issue (such as discrimination).

But the literature reveals the story. Grievance procedures are aimed to protect employees and restore justice, but can and do exacerbate the problem with punishments for filing in the first place. Typical studies show that a year or so after a personal grievance, the filers have lower performance ratings and promotion rates but higher turnover figures. Not a lot of forgive and forget, more learn and move on here!

Governments and businesses all encourage decentralized dispute resolution processes at the workplace level, so that earlier low-level (read 'non-escalating') resolution might occur.

It's clearly best to have a workplace conflict management procedure and system that everyone understands and thinks is fair. But who designs the system, and in whose interests? A management system may be very different from a union-based one.

Oh dear – more systems, more expense, more bureaucracy. Feels like that, until you have a nasty grievance case on your hands that poisons the whole office or production line. Best be prepared, best know what to expect and what to do. Too late if you have to grieve about not having a good grievance procedure.

I. HOW 'FAMILY FRIENDLY' CAN BACKFIRE

A productive and loyal employee comes to you with two requests. You know she is a passionate dog- lover and breeder and has four thoroughbreds. She asks for time off to take two of them to the vet. And also wants an afternoon off to take them to an all-important show.

She loves the dogs, talks about them the whole time, displays their pictures. They mean a lot to her. And she is a good employee. What do you say? 'Just this once as a special favour' or 'It's not part of company policy.' What if you don't like dogs – will that influence your decision? And what will the work group make of it?

Now replace dogs with children. A mother with four wants/has to take young children to the doctor/dentist. She would also love to go to their sports day or prize-giving. Now what do you say?

There are pet-friendly pubs, hotels, resorts. There are also those which discreetly advertise that their establishment and resort is child free. It is for adults only; not (you understand, doctor) as in 'adult entertainment'. But it guarantees (you hope) less noise, litter, anti-social behaviour.

The fundamental issue here is the unintended consequences of a company's family-friendly policies. For a long time now work–life balance and family-friendly policies have been high on the corporate agenda. Usually driven by the female-dominated HR department, family friendly is seen as a fundamental issue that suits the zeitgeist. The lite version is called work–life balance . . . but that includes other issues.

Many (male) managers question the wisdom of what they see as 'letting some people off work' on a regular basis. Some may secretly even prefer to stay at work where they feel more in control, more powerful and more supported than they are when they get home and are expected to do a whole range of tedious and demeaning domestic duties.

Ready for the attack, enthusiasts for family-friendly policies quote their favourite research. They may never have read (or critiqued) it and perhaps 'bought' the conclusions from an earnest consultant in these matters, but

they sure know the bottom line. Family-friendly policies, they assure us, lead to more and better applicants,
greater retention, higher satisfaction, more productivity.
In short, your bottom liners have the evidence you need.
Family friendly is a really good investment.

The cynical and sceptical manager may doubt this,
but faced with a confident chapter-and-verse HR (sorry,
Talent Management) professionals, may reluctantly
back down. He may, however, employ a researcher to
do a critique of some of this work. We all know how
difficult these things are to measure. And are there really
good studies using a 'before' (no policy) and 'after' (with
policy). Studies with a *proper control group*. And how
can you know it is this policy that is working (and for
how long) and not something else? Is it a placebo, a
Hawthorne effect, a mirage?

In fact, stories from some companies report the opposite of the expected positive effect. The answer lies in the
demography of the staff. Imagine you are in a close-knit,
mutually dependent work group. It's pretty mixed – some
older people (over 50) and some younger (under 25).
And there are those with children who benefit from the
family-friendly policies. They are entitled to more temporal flexibility. They are allowed to take time off for the
children's special events – rites of passage – stuff.

But how do the older people, who never benefited
from these enlightened policies when they were parents
of young children, feel? Can they make up and have the
same flexibility for their grandchildren? What about the
unmarried, the child-free, the not-yet-there? Can they go
to their cousin's sports day, or help out their sister with
her children?

The issue is the F-word: fairness. Actually it is the
E-word: equitable. Why are some people deserving of
special treatment? Because they have young children and
we want people with young children to work here. But is
their contribution the same? Who covers for them when

they are away? What happens when all the parents on the staff put in for the same weeks of leave (school holidays, half term?)

Clearly there are those who are equity sensitive. They argue, with obviously a cocktail of mixed motives and emotions, that if people choose to breed they must be prepared to pay the price. Others are quite happy to share the burden 'for the benefit of society'. And what of the rights of fathers? Just as we have maternity leave and now paternity leave, should all these family-friendly benefits be extended to fathers?

Perhaps in some organizations, where staff with young families are in the majority, family-friendly policies may succeed. In others, where they are seen as a minority, the enmity of staff not entitled to perceived 'unfair privileges' could be too great a cost to bear.

It's the law of unintended consequences stuff again. In trying to be kind and helpful, one stirs great resentment and wrath. All hopes for the bottom line go out of the window and disengaged, non-family, unfriendly staff show their displeasure through their poor attendance and productivity.

J. LEGISLATION AND REGULATION

The departments that are most loathed in organizations are those that insist on us following seemingly pointless, restricting and intrusive rules. *HR*, *Health and Safety*, and *Security* seem to do little else but send out memos dictating how things are to be done. They are natural regulators whose primary aim is to draw up policies, rules and regulations that affect everybody all the time.

Of course, they have many rationalizations for their rule impositions. Security people say it is all for our own safety, while Occupational Health go on and on about accident prevention. HR usually dishe up some pretty dodgy 'state-of-the-art', 'cutting edge', or 'breakthrough' research which demonstrates, quite equivocally, that job satisfaction and productivity are strongly linked to some process that we are required to follow.

Looking back, it is often clear how stupid some of these restrictions were.

Lawyers are naturally to be found behind many of these edits. Most ethical committees have much less to do with ethics than they do with litigation. Similarly, appraisal schemes are more about the fear of losing 'unfair dismissal' court cases than good management. In fact, the more people are dragooned and restricted in their behaviour at work, the more scheming they become in breaking the rules, just as more taxes lead to more accountants.

Some security people have learnt to their cost that introducing cameras, swipe cards and no-go areas have led to such resentment that they have encouraged the very behaviours (theft, sabotage, arson, fraud) they were trying to reduce. Equally, the more process-driven appraisals become, the more both sides agree to fiddle the paperwork. Some systems grow so complex that managers are given manuals running to hundreds of pages on how to rate their employees. One consultant received a great accolade by burning all the HR manuals in the garden to demonstrate the need for simplicity.

New-rule-making seems to be the top concern of politicians. This may be because so many are lawyers and educators. They have not only the 'gift of the gab' but also a peculiar interest in making rules that others have to follow.

The aspect of managerialism that is always most disliked and despised is the urge to impose restrictions and insist on conformity, irrespective of its consequences on staff morale or indeed organizational profitability. Worse, we all know about the *law of unintended consequences*, where legislators exacerbate rather than cure existing problems.

The explanations for the introduction of the rules are usually PC flim-flammery, rather than having a sound economic base. It is as if 'health and safety' or personal security are criteria in their own right.

Some governments seem to believe their only power lies in introducing new laws. How many new taxes did the last government introduce? Yet, again and again there are calls for simplification of the tax system.

The recent issue concerning security at airports illustrates the point perfectly. Many of the security checks are pointless. Did Mr Bin Laden have shares in security firms? He certainly helped them. Not only do the procedures annoy and humiliate passengers, they also delay planes. The costs are astronomical. There are redundant systems. But the security experts, of course, disagree. Restricting, fleecing and corralling people comes naturally to them . . . all for your own security of course. They always say that . . . particularly in nasty, undemocratic regimes.

Once in place, legislation has a dead-hand effect. But not any more! Hurrah for freedom, common sense and liberty. There are new government legislation slogans that we could do well to apply to business:

One in, one out: This means you can't add anything without first taking something away. You can have new rules as long as others are revoked. In some ways this means the rule book can change, but it can't get longer. It means having to prioritize and not just add stuff. What is really important is that it makes people re-examine what is truly relevant and what can be discarded.

Sell-by-date legislation: This means any and all legislation runs out after a certain period and needs to be re-introduced through the whole process once more. Nothing lasts forever. Some laws and rules backfire badly. Anyone working in an office knows about this: rules designed to reduce work more often increase it.

There are wonderful examples in this country where laws, once possibly sensible, lived on way past their sell-by date. Pubs used to close in the afternoon as a result of First World War legislation regarding munitions factories. Children still have long school summer holidays to help bring in the harvest. Perhaps we need a few retired lawyers to go through the statutes and remove, or justify daft, outdated legislation.

Sunsetting regulators: This means all regulators, whoever they are, have a fixed term, non-renewable appointment. You have a set period of office: none of this president-for-life nonsense that you see in banana republics. No re-election, extension. The fact that a post has a fixed life should concentrate the mind. To some extent it could encourage manic rule-passing, but the above two restrictions might limit that behaviour. It should in some way sharpen the senses: how to leave your mark in the time that is available.

K. MEMORY AND VISION

In some cultures the chameleon is a deeply feared animal. Not for its ability to change colour, nor for the speed, accuracy and length of its razor tongue. It is because its eyes can move independently. Indeed, it can look in two directions at once. Focus on the past and the future at the same time.

Consider the contrast between memory and vision – where we came from and where we are going. Some people, at any age, are happiest when looking back. Like historians, they believe they can understand the future best by looking at the past. By contrast, some people are so future-oriented that they cannot endure sitting in a train facing backwards. For them the past is another forgotten country. It is the destination, not the origin that is important. The trick is the mixing and fusion of the story of where we came from and also where we are going.

It is not only the old who look back and the young who look forward. Nor only the successful who dwell on the past and the less successful who wish to forget it. Nor is it some optimism vs pessimism issue. It is more about those who can see the journey in its entirety.

Organizations that often have the most difficulty changing are those with a long and successful past. There is deep memory. Glorious tales of success. Old photographs. Lovingly preserved artefacts of some golden period. Educational institutions do it well, as do family-owned businesses. It is like changing the direction of a fully laden oil tanker.

It's much easier to change and manage a new business organization. And it's perhaps even easier to manage a failed one. In the former we make the rules as we go along. In the latter what was tried, failed – so things have to be done differently. Perhaps this is why cynical and manipulative (or are they just wise?) CEOs sometimes engineer crises to bring about change.

One way to mix memory and vision is to distort memory. One only has to go to an old school reunion to be surprised, not at how much but at how little people have (really) changed, save the grey hair, wrinkles and weight gain, and also how their memories of your time together differ. They remember the same events differently as well as having quite different memory stores. The same teacher was a tyrant to some, to the others an inspiration. For some it was a bullying culture, for others a supportive, caring culture.

Memory is a cohort issue. People in the same cohort (Baby Boomers, Millennials, etc.) seem to share values and memories. One cohort's glorious past seems mildly shabby and disappointing to the next. Customs and values change, and therein should lie hope. Moreover, corporate memories are often deliberately manipulated by organizations. There are many symbols of victories, be it profitable years to the openings of great buildings, but little reference to the future.

The memory issue can be vividly seen in organizations that require a serious rebranding and realignment. In some there is a Pol Pot-like destruction of the memory of the past. Just as the shock troops of reformist, Puritan, Protestant England destroyed the monasteries and icons of what they saw as corrupt Catholicism, so modern-day reformers destroy all symbols of the past. Badges, even photographs, are banned with serious consequences. See post-war impositions on the Nazis.

Organizations with a memory have certain advantages. It can give them a great brand to exploit for years. It can help give coherence to a company. People choose to work there and buy products and services because they think they know what they are getting. But, equally, such organizations can very soon look very old fashioned – dinosaurs of the past, ill-adapted to the world of today.

We know the (business) world is an ever-changing, complex and competitive place. We know the world does not need your permission to change. We have heard it all before. So we need a map, a plan, a strategy that tells us about destinations and routes. But we also know, of course, there is no destination – just markers on the journey.

Some unlikely organizations, such as hotels and hospitals, employ archivists to preserve their history. Others commission histories which show some bias. At anniversaries there may be great celebrations. After all, survival needs to be celebrated. It's about fitness indeed.

The problem does not (yet) exist for new companies. Hugely successful companies (like Apple, Google and Microsoft) don't have much of a past. Such folklore that does exist tends to relate to the CEO founder who is still in charge and benefits from the story.

So why don't all older organizations have someone in charge of their history – a Chief Memory Officer. It would be their job to manage the past. True, they might not sit on the board or receive a very high salary, but this is not to demean their role. This is to align the past with the future. They might manage the past by telling stories. Selective memory that aids the future.

Blending the past and the future is not easy.

L. PAPER TRAIL CULTURE

Anyone who has to face, in any capacity, a work tribunal (or, indeed, a Commons Select Committee) soon begins to become very conscious of the value of the paper trail. And yes, it is still called that – in the electronic age of the paperless office, we need paper trails.

What is meant by a paper trail is essentially sequential evidence. Evidence on paper or email that appraisals were held, warnings were given, statements were made. Lawyers have learnt how to have a field day humiliating the senior manager or emotional employee whose only 'data' or evidence is the memory of some (traumatic) event. The 'my word against yours' philosophy soon looks pretty pathetic.

People learn, often after some costly (in every sense) experience, to 'take and keep' notes. All those who give advice, deal with the public or manage others learn to do this. Teachers and doctors, managers and coaches, indeed practically anybody who deals with the public (who sometimes treat complaining as a new, rewarding Olympic sport) need to learn to gather evidence.

Failure to do so, as BBC editors have found, can mean that a '10-second conversation during lunch' will return to haunt you many months later.

The evidence needs to be detailed. In fact, some organizations provide 'record sheets' to help keep professional records of all the salient details of a meeting: date and time, others present, agreements entered into. Some even require that these are signed.

Don't all meetings begin with a request that the minutes of the last meeting are agreed? It's so common and tedious that little or no attention is paid to this ritual. As a consequence, highly savvy managers learn to subtly doctor the really important bits lest they arise in a later hearing. Did not everybody agree that the minutes were an accurate record of what was said? As a bit of fun, try challenging the minutes at your next meeting and see all the confusion that follows.

But some organizations have turned paper trailing into an art form. The *cover your backside, put it in print, document all events* culture has to be seen to be experienced. Dare one suggest that it is found *much* more in the public, as opposed to the private, sector? Imagine a Silicon Valley Group of entrepreneurs, inventors and boffins keeping records of all the meetings they go to. Indeed, by contrast, imagine the number of meetings that civil servants attend that are not extremely heavy on paper trails.

Is it possible to characterize people, and the organizations in which they work, as being at one extreme paper-trail-obsessive and at the other paper-trail-phobic? The obsessives are record-keeping documenters who aim to capture and record everything that is done, said, proposed, and delivered by others. They are *Hansardists, archivists, documenters* of events. Indeed, many are so busy taking notes, they seem to have little time for anything else. It can take as long to write up the minutes of a meeting than to run it in the first place. So much so that some organizations employ people to be paper trailers: the 'Secretary to the Board' as was. That is their exclusive function.

To the paper-trail-phobic this is amazing, pointless, counterproductive behaviour. Life is too short both to stuff a mushroom and to minute every meeting that is held. Some believe in the 'my word is my bond' philosophy, though that terminology seems pretty old-fashioned.

To some the philosophy and culture of the standing-up, water-cooler-moment meeting with an agreement at the end is enough. Appraisals can be held in airport lounges, hotel bars and trains. As long as the central message gets across, that is all that is required. We are here to make money, not to take notes.

Most people and organizations are somewhere 'in the middle'. But it does not take a lot to shift the centre towards the obsessive. Wait until you have a complaint of bullying behaviour or an unfair dismissal case. Wait until you have to provide evidence of the appraisal or the 'heated meeting'.

Wait until you have to call in an IT specialist to try to recover some email from two years ago that said something about having a meeting to resolve issues. This may be the only 'paper-trail' evidence you can obtain to prove that an event was at least planned, even if it did not happen.

So how to cover your backside without breaking the bank? How to ensure there is *enough* paper-trail activity to protect you from adverse events? First, log the more important stuff. Have a box, icon or whatever, where you store records of meetings and interchanges. Times and dates and who is present is minimal. Maybe add the agenda and the few most important agreed/disagreed points/then cc to all present for comments, feedback, additions.

Second, look out for difficult people, departments and issues. They are worth special attention. Call them trouble makers, rule followers, due-diligence people or whatever. They can and do cause trouble. Beware and prepare. Anticipate paper-trail obsession. It is worth taking a bit of time over this.

Third, consider other types of recorded evidence. Richard Nixon no doubt rued the day he tape-recorded all conversations in the White House. There are surveillance methods (cameras, lights, locks) that keep records of behaviour. Of course, they bring their own problems, but they can be cheap and efficient ways of taking over from paper-trail obsessionality.

M. PRIORITIZATION

Market research has shown that people want four things from their supermarkets: competitive pricing (value for money), ease of getting what they want (selection), clear aisles (ease of shopping) and helpful staff (service). 'Bleeding obvious' as the Pythons might observe. Yes, but with two caveats: rank order and trade-off.

While few would disagree about the desirability of these different markers of a good supermarket, the question is: what is most important to customers and what are they prepared to trade off? Lidl is different from Waitrose; Iceland from Harrods. For some, price is all – little choice, off-hand and inattentive staff, crowding, but a real deal.

Others want a serious choice of extra-virgin olive oil, organic coffee or every type of pesto. They are prepared to pay if the product is right. Another group – let's call them 'men' – want the transaction to be as quick as possible. They are hunter-gatherers, happy to be out of the shop faster than you can say, 'Did you bring your own bags?' Easy-to-find stuff, no queues and they are prepared to pay a fortune.

And then there are those who like to feel special. Shopping is a social occasion where they want to find engaged staff who are happy in their work and very willing to march you off to find the vanilla essence or the Angostura bitters, which seems to be misfiled.

So the price-insensitive, cash-rich, time-poor shopper has very different needs from the good-value shopper. And it's not difficult to see. Everything about the Lidl shopper, from their dress to their gait, differentiates them from people at the Waitrose cheese counter.

Perhaps the same four factors apply to airlines. Assuming that safety is a given, we all search for a cheap ticket to a desirable destination on an uncrowded plane with schedule choice and charming staff. Not too difficult to see the trade-off issues here. Compare Ryanair to Singapore Airlines. Thanks to the CEO of Ryanair, who is renowned for his straight talking, you know what the 'value proposition is'. It's pretty clear and there is a lot to trade off.

Consider the time, price, and quality trade-off when hiring a trades' person for a piece of work. If it's quick and cheap, you sacrifice quality. If its quick and good quality, you pay. If its high-quality workmanship at a competitive price, you wait your turn. So what will you sacrifice and for what? Despite ads and promises to the contrary, there is no such thing as all three: having your cake and eating it.

Is the same issue not true in the workplace? Not difficult to come up with a list of things you want from a job. First, there are all the 'comp and ben' staff, remuneration, salary, dosh. Few would not rate this highly. As much as possible. Second, there is something to do with the hours, pressure, stress. Some jobs are physically demanding, others intellectually demanding and still others emotionally demanding. Within reason, people don't want to have their 'resources' stretched on a daily basis to meet the demands of the job. Third, there are the interpersonals: how you get on with your boss, colleagues, reports and customers. Hell, and joy, is other people. For how long and how much are you prepared to put up with a bullying boss, back-stabbing peers and surly staff? Or consistently abusive, demanding customers?

Fourth, what about job security (if there is such a thing anymore)? What is it worth being a casual labourer at the whim of the market with a week's notice. Of course, there are other factors as well. Some people genuinely want to do work which benefits others in the community. Here ideology is the driver. Others want jobs which really help them develop their skill set, which play and nurture their talents and allow them to self-actualize. For some, geographical factors are important – they want to stay working in a particular region.

People make these choices early on in their lives. Few (really) highly paid jobs come without great demands. So what are you prepared to 'put up with' for £200K or £500K. Very (very) long hours, taxing work, and less-than-supportive colleagues. A job where you can be 'out-on-your-ear' for a minor slip-up. And where in a public life you are met by a mixture of contempt and envy.

And what would you give for a lovely, warm and supportive boss, and kind, helpful and fun colleagues and customers who seem appreciative of what you give them? How much is that worth?

What is tenure (the idea that it is very difficult to sack you or make you redundant) worth? What value does security have, or is that really little more than a myth, an idea or ideal from another world?

The trouble with the trade-off idea is that things have changed. It used to be assumed that you traded off high pay for job security and service above self-ideals if you worked in the public sector. The private sector was more challenging and competitive – read stressful and vicious – and certainly less secure, but you had better pay.

And how things have changed. People in the private sector look aghast at the salaries of public-service bureaucrats with high pension pots and other perks. Perhaps the stereotype was never true. And the trade-off issue is always in flux and dynamic. Perhaps there are secure, highly paid jobs that are not so demanding and populated with jolly, helpful and supportive people. If they are there at the end of the rainbow, do let me know.

N. SLAUGHTER OF THE INNOCENTS

Those interested in politics in the workplace have sometimes mapped out the territory with various typologies. These are usually described on two dimensions unrelated to each other, yielding four boxes. The boxes contain the prototypic types.

There are problems with typologies. They are crude, and people at extremes within the box can be quite different. Typologies often don't explain how people ended up in a particular box, or the fundamental processes that explain observable behaviours.

The favoured dimensions for the 'politics-at-work' people are *politically aware/unaware* and *acting with/ without integrity*. They can't quite bring themselves to use the term 'psychological game playing'. The boxes are given labels, which are far from value free. Always one of the two labels on a particular dimension is implicitly and explicitly the better.

So, for politics the four types are called *Wise* (political savvy, has integrity), *Innocent* (no savvy but has integrity), *Inept* (no savvy, no integrity) and *Clever* (savvy, no integrity).

The people who are categorized in the optimally good (wise) and bad (inept) boxes are the least interesting. It is almost inconceivable to imagine how the Inept ever get anywhere in life. They seem too dim and dishonest; blindly egocentric; clumsily childlike. They appear, if anything, to be Kevin-the-Teenager narcissistic adolescents – all hormones and no grey cells. Difficult to imagine in which organizations they can possibly thrive.

Equally, there is the improbability of the Wise owl. The humane, skilled, supportive uber-heroes. They are the ultimate emotionally intelligent, ethical and insightful leaders – the Cecil B. DeMille religious prophet, the grey-templed benefactor, the selfless servant-leader. They are the good guys of course. They are tactful and loyal, open and ethical, perceptive and receptive. They are non-defensive and can cope with being disliked. They know how to get the best out of people and have a win-win mentality. In short, they understand the foibles of the human condition.

But the really interesting types are those with only half of what is required. First, the power-hungry, rather dodgy Clever types. Read the descriptors and these people appear somewhere between *psychopathic* and *Machiavellian*. They have a veneer of charm and leave jobs before their mistakes are discovered. They can make the process and procedures work for them. They are observant and happy to exploit the weaknesses and setbacks of both allies and opponents. They know when to bargain, ingratiate, simulate and manipulate.

They are not called 'clever' for no reason. Would it be wrong or unfair to suggest that these people possess exactly what you need to make it to the top? Shrewd, perceptive, savvy people who know how organizations and people tick. They don't need influence or negotiation skills courses; they have all those skills in place. Add a dash of ambition, good looks and intellectual ability and you get the modern CEO.

Perhaps the most interesting are the Innocents. How did they come to be like that and how can they be helped before they are slaughtered? These people play by the rules. They are respectful of rank and position. They believe what they are told. They pride themselves in their rationality.

Innocents don't network or gossip. They don't read between the lines. They are not psychologically minded and are often neither interested in, nor very able to understand the complex and dark motives of others.

Just as autistic people can't read emotions in others, so innocents can't seem to understand their motives. They have are childlike with respect to their fellow man. And they get left behind at work. Easy targets for the Machiavellians above, below and beside them.

So how can you help the Innocents? How do you teach political savvy and awareness? Read psychology books or novels? Usually the playground is the first setting for learning political savvy. Children don't always tell the truth and they are often selfish and cruel. It's best to be part of a gang, a group, a support network for mutual help. It is important to know how to deal with bullies and even admirers. Some people are more touchy and sensitive than others. You need to know how to avoid or deal with problematic situations.

There are courses aimed at developing political skills. Some organizations will have nothing to do with them or else try to change their title. Politics is seen as underhand, dirty, devious. Of course it can be.

Courses on selling are sometimes seen as manipulative, even immoral. Salespeople use psychological knowledge and tricks to bamboozle people and deprive them of their hard-earned cash. Or do they simply apply legal techniques to influence others?

People who need to develop political skills require two courses: one on motivation and the other on persuasion. They need to understand how basic human motives for recognition, power or pleasure are manifest and how complicated they can be. They also need to learn a few skills and techniques of influence.

Being political does not mean being corrupt (necessarily). It is a crucial skill set. Those who can't or won't acquire it are usually condemned to be, at best, observers of the game of life or victims of those who know how to play the rules.

O. VIOLENCE AT WORK

The stats really are alarming. Based on data from 10 European countries, 22 per cent of nurses claimed in a survey to have experienced a direct violent episode (verbal and physical) from patients and relatives.

In Britain the figure was nearly 80 per cent in accident and emergency, 60 per cent in mental health settings and 50 per cent in wards for the elderly. There are around 60,000 reports of physical assaults in the NHS every year. And the financial costs have been estimated to be around £60 million.

But it is not only people in medicine and social care who report workplace violence. There are, increasingly, reports from education and transportation sectors. Equally, there are problems in the hotel and catering, and retail sectors. It is not uncommon to witness considerable verbal abuse in waiting rooms of many kinds, be they at airports, hospitals or railway stations.

Priests are attacked and murdered. Shop assistants report constant verbal abuse by customers unhappy to wait for their turn.

And it's not always drunk yobs, feral children or callous aggressive adults who shout, scream and occasionally lunge out at serving staff. The tired, frustrated, middle-class executive has been known to let off steam.

TV programmes set in airports – 'Airport' (BBC) and 'Airline' (ITV) – show how amazingly rude and unreasonable ordinary people can be when kept waiting or not having their wishes met. Indeed airports, with all the excitement and stress associated with travel, seem particularly prone to violence.

The serious questions are about cause and cure. What causes workplace, public aggression and what can be done about it? Is it getting worse or better? Are there cultural differences or universals? For years the accident literature has divided causes into two broad areas: those caused by systems design and failures, and those caused by individual volitions and errors.

It is possible that some customer violence is caused by the organization itself. The constant breakdown of equipment due to poor maintenance, understaffing due to poor management causing massive absenteeism, having rules and procedures that serve little purpose other than to wind people up. Organizational rules and procedures are essentially the cause.

Most (public) organizations will explain any of these problems in terms of funding. No money, thus fewer, less experienced, younger staff leading to angry, demanding, entitled and aggressive customers. Yes, it is organizational not individual, but we (the management) are not to blame.

The second explanation lies in the personality of those who exhibit violence. These types are then split into the pathological and moral. So, if you want pathological labels, there are disorders known as 'psychopathic/callousness' or 'passive-aggressivenss explosion'. On the other hand, it may be just as satisfying to provide some moral labels such as 'selfish ego-centrism' or 'thoughtless reaction', or simply 'bad manners'.

Diagnosing the cause of violence, of course, has implications for the cure or intervention. Reduction of violence against staff may require changing organizational work practices, policies and procedures, deciding emergency action plans, and providing group or individual training programmes to teach workers how to deal with aggressive episodes and their consequences.

If you intend to train people, what do they need to know? Presumably the legal issues as well as the organization's policy, procedures and practices as regards to workplace aggression and violence. They may also need some help and practice with physical intervention (breakaway, control and restraint techniques) as well as the verbal stuff. Equally, it may be helpful to have some idea of how best to cope with the emotional upset and shock afterwards.

It is useful to be very clear about a definition – what exactly is work-related aggression and violence? Not a bad idea to have a simple but functional model for understanding when/how/why violence occurs. This helps identify early warning signs.

People can be taught physical and verbal strategies that successfully de-escalate violence before it becomes too serious.

And they need to know how to submit a report afterwards which is salient, unambiguous and useful for authority.

Employees are most frightened and vulnerable when they are alone or on a night shift, or if the perpetrators of the violence are in groups, under the influence of drugs or on some emotional high.

Training targeted at individuals may undermine what may be called collective capability for dealing with aggression. People need to feel their organization will be supportive and sympathetic and try to prevent a recurrence. They need to feel that they and their colleagues are properly trained to deal with any problems that may arise.

The bottom line is fairly clear. Workplace violence has an impact on personal well-being, morale and productivity. Yet the evidence is that training programmes have limited value and that their effects wear off over time. There are really three reasons for this: First, course content is often not that relevant to individual needs. Second, training is too 'feel good' rather than skill based. Third, the cause does not concentrate on making individuals and groups feel more competent and capable at dealing with the issues.

Most organizations soon find that the cost of ignoring workplace violence is much greater than trying to deal with it effectively.

P. WILL POWER

The three great monotheistic religions have much in common, despite their obvious differences and mutual antipathy. The People-of-the-Book have set periods of denial where will power is tested.

What have *Lent, Ramadan and Yom Kippur* have in common? Three things: First, the well-known concept of *abstinence and self-denial*. This is most often associated with foods – foods that one gives up for Lent (chocolate, meat, alcohol) or feeding during the hours of daylight. They demand fasting for 40 days or at least 25 hours. Food is a good target because of the constant reminders of the season. Some rules are stricter than others: *nil by mouth* is the strongest form of the decree. Fasting is easier for shorter periods and apparently very good for you, but the lengthy Ramadan period may lead to health problems.

The second theme of this period is *repentance and penitence* for one's sins of omission and commission. It is a time to look back and try to make amends. Also, to try to reset the compass, strive to be better. The third theme is *charity*. It is time to think more about others, to be grateful and to share one's blessings.

It seems for most of us in this post-religious, quasi-atheistic time period, that New Year has come to replace the great religious festivals. New Year resolutions are not framed in terms of penance and giving, but as a new start, a new opportunity. Most resolutions are about eating and drinking less, exercising more and generally being less selfish and nice to people. Watch the television advertisements to get a sense of what it is all about. Health clubs, nicotine patches, alcohol-free drinks get a good airing.

Christmas is all about spoiling yourself and others ('because you are worth it') while New Year is all about restraint. As Robbie Williams in his song 'Millennium' sang, '. . . overdose at Christmas and give it up in Lent'.

So, the old Lent ritual begins with Shrove Tuesday and pancakes, the Ash Wednesday and the start of the season of solemnity, simplicity and sincerity. And 40 days is a long time. It is a test of will power. Of course there is a sort of half time called 'Refreshment Sunday', which means a little acceptable indulgence.

Psychologists are particularly interested in will power and the power of self-control. For Roy Baumeister, an American social psychologist, it is, as the subtitle of his new book states, the *Greatest Human Strength*. Practically all the problems of modern society that plague us – from debt to domestic violence, and unwanted pregnancy to underperformance at school and work – can (at least in part) be attributable to will power. He argues that two things bring multiple benefits in life: intelligence and will power. You need both. There's not much you can do about the former, but you can improve the latter.

But will power is a limited resource, as we all know. We get 'will power depletion'. We get exhausted resisting desires and temptations. But the good news is that self-control is like a muscle – the more we exercise, the better we become at not giving into temptations that lead to idleness, and illness.

Most of us know about will power depletion. After a day facing bolshy customers or difficult appraises, it is a problem not to go home and open a bottle of good claret or enjoy a tempting canapé. This comfort eating, hitting the bottle, even retail therapy is an attempt at restoration of the spirit. One is just too pooped to follow the plan.

That is why it is easier to resist temptation in the wilderness, as JC found. A monastery, a retreat, an isolated Scottish or Welsh cottage is so much easier than the hubbub of business life. Quite simply, to have the best shot at will power, training needs to be secluded and calm. Go to a health farm, have a walking away-day.

So, how about some company policies around this issue? Don't mention religion because that only causes 'stuff' as we have recently seen. Let's start with some assumptions: People with will power at work are better employees. They resist temptations better and more often and, as a result, produce more. They do better under pressure and can be trusted to complete the task. They are less vulnerable to all the temptations of excess.

So what can organizations do to help those attempting to beef up their self-control muscles during the Lent period? The first is to select for and reward will power. Call it 'grit' or 'determination' or 'self-control'. It is what middle-class parents try to inculcate in their young because they know it serves them well. So put temptation out of sight. Make sure all rewards fit the self-control theme.

Q. WORKING FROM HOME

Work is something you do, not a place you go to. The possibility of working *at* or *from* home is growing ever more simple and, for both employer and worker, more attractive. Indeed, the Olympic Games might, for Londoners, have proven to be a time to do some excellent experimental work as they were encouraged to stay put, but online.

The online bit is important. Online to what, or to whom? Online to the web, to databases, to reports? Does it have to be online to people? If you read accounts of writers, scientists, artists, designers – people who have to spend a lot of time 'just thinking' – the web seems less than essential. Indeed a possible distraction. But that is another story . . .

The distinction between working *at* home and *from* home is important. The latter implies considerably more contact and communication than the former. Indeed, is this not the rationale for going to work in the first place? The workplace offers constant face-to-face communication (via various channels) that facilitates quick and accurate feedback, as well as a sense of common ground, connection and mutuality.

Theoretically, propinquity and proximity lead to more and better information sharing, which is the cornerstone both of productivity and satisfaction. So, the logic proceeds, the home teleworker, having reduced opportunities for quality communication (even shooting the breeze), feels isolated, cut off and marginalized. And this mood state is hardly ideal for productive work.

Yet the invention of teleworking was now so long ago that researchers have a good body of data with which to study the whole teleworker experience. They have found, somewhat predictably, a curvilinear relationship between telework and satisfaction. Those with no teleworking hours and those with only teleworking hours showed the least satisfaction. A little of the experience seemed optimal.

So the communications experts looked at the real value of 'being there'. Is face-to-face communication that beneficial? Is there any advantage of keeping people at their distance? Various ideas have been proposed.

The first may worry some managers. It is the idea of work–life conflict. Teleworkers manage this better, possibly by working less. Not so, cry the parents who are prepared to put in the hours, but at times to suit the family timetable. Not so, says the commuter whose place of abode is dependent on their partner's work and children's school. The commute is exhausting, expensive and an unnecessary strain on energy and money. But there is always that lingering doubt.

Of course, just as there is work–life conflict, so there is life–work conflict, which is the idea that one's personal lifestyle and circumstances interfere with work activity.

Next, there is the real problem of interruptions. Endless meetings and the like in the workplace, which are serious distractions. The office yields everyday unexpected conversations, telephone calls, 'urgent' emails, background noise and the call for meetings. All stressful and time-wasting, particularly for introverts or those whose work involves serious concentration.

Working at home means one is less exposed to office politics. Less gossip, less need to avoid certain people, to fake behaviour to others and to decode complex symbols. Do you have to fake getting along to get ahead? Do you have to work at being a favourite, an 'in-crowd' member to get promotion? Do you have to keep quiet on important issues for fear of retaliation? There are serious distractions in the workplace, but being outside the loop for too long could also mean being sidelined in important promotion, restructuring or other decisions.

Good communication is about clear, efficient information exchange. Why is a face-to-face conversation necessarily better than an email? Surely it depends on the subtlety of what is being said, and most day-to-day stuff is not that full of innuendo, dissimulation or coded messages.

Teleworkers do tend to interact with their colleagues less. This can be both a good and a bad thing. It may be that they save communications (telephone, emails) for when messages are really important. Teleworkers are also less interrupted by garrulous time-wasting colleagues who produce very little. The cost is less connectedness, but that can be a good thing.

Who said face-to-face interactions always (even often) produce positive outcomes? Teleworking enhances autonomy, flexibility and the ability to concentrate. It allows more filtering of information and a reduction in superfluous conversations.

So, are high-intensity teleworkers more productive and satisfied? How to persuade the sceptical manager that all this telework is not just an excuse for less work? It's not that difficult to conceive of a study what would test the idea, as long as one could measure productivity well: A group of workers are selected. They spend three months at work, three months at home, three months doing half and half. One lets them get used to it. Then you start to measure productivity. Any changes? What direction? Are there job differences? What about the all-important control group who stay the same. A PhD proposal, anyone?

The modern worker is confronted with information overload. Email fatigue is common. People ask for quiet time, quiet rooms, quiet coaches to ensure temporal, physical and technological boundaries that allow them to concentrate.

People yearn for quiet, safe spaces to ponder stuff. For some it is the canteen, but equally the local park. All places to be yourself, to think things through, to be creative. To be away from the onslaught and the tyranny of the 'urgent'.

The future is digital. Offices are expensive; commuting is difficult. There will be more and more teleworkers, often in remote locations or abroad, whom both managers and customers may not meet.

R. SOCIAL NETWORKING

Facebook or LinkedIn? Rotary Club or the Lions? Reform or Athenaeum? You need connections in life. Networking works. Are business cards old hat?

Should you join the Twitterati (whether you have something interesting to say or not)? Or is it like in the old days, when it was rather impressive to have a telephone number that 'wasn't in the book'. Ex-directory. The message was: don't call us, we'll call you. Being hard to get at was good.

Social networking is in. Be there or be square. Today's communication is electronic. It is all about computer-mediated connectivity. But is this little more than a young person's narcissistic toy? Are the messages trivial, egocentric and deeply incoherent?

What does the middle-aged business person need to know and do when faced with the social media? Are real grown-ups on Facebook? What does it mean if you refuse an invitation to being connected on LinkedIn? Is it a case of join in or lose out?

The media experts and psychologists have caught up and conducted some interesting studies on social media such as Facebook. Established in 2004, it now has 750 million active members across the globe. This perhaps most trafficked of sites across the world has made its founder very rich. But is Facebook a good thing? Has it made young people isolated, dependent and less socially skilled than they otherwise might be?

Are social media only for young people? Well pretty much, partly due to young uns' adeptness at navigating the Web and them being generally computer savvy. Is it for the more or less sociable? Are users nervous introverts, finding it the only way to make friends, or do anxious people avoid it because they are concerned about the open nature of the information? Do those who have stronger needs to belong join social media groups to feed their sense of inclusion? Indeed, isn't the number of friends you have on Facebook a sign of your popularity? A bit like counting the number of Christmas cards you receive?

Or, more darkly, is this in fact ersatz sociability? Does virtual interaction replace real interaction, leading to the development of a vicious cycle? So, less is more. It is all about quality not quantity? Who, not how many.

Curiously, although a number of studies have tested the above, perfectly reasonable hypothesis, few have found it to hold water. There is no strong connection between personality and social media usage. Perhaps there are other factors that are more important.

So what do social media users get out of it? Cheap and quick communication? A harmless diversion from everyday life? A way to develop and boost personal identity? The building of a virtual network? A way of keeping in touch and up-to-date with old and new friends? Maybe a hint of status seeking? Or a sort of social browsing?

Why do, or should, organizations use Facebook? Three years after it started, it 'allowed' corporations to develop a platform. Within 24 hours, 100,000 organizations had created a profile. Many saw it as a clever and cheap way of encouraging (particularly young people) engagement with, becoming a fan of, and extending the brand. So we now have well over three million brand identities, supported by 20 million fans. It has been seen as a (if not *the*) most important customer relationship management tool for corporations and marketers. Punters can communicate with brands and have a relationship with some or other aspect of them.

It has been suggested that Facebook can really help PR, particularly in times of crisis where it can be used as a management and damage mitigation tool. Equally, consumers can spread bad news about an organization if they wish. It really is, as Citizen Smith noted, 'power to the people'.

Companies can conduct very cheap market research using social media. If nothing else, Facebook and other social media provide a cheap and efficient platform by which to contact many people all around the world.

But what about the issue of subterfuge, dishonesty and fantasy for Facebook users? Exaggerated, idealized essentially dishonest identities can be presented for a range of motives. Self-promotion and narcissism – often delusional? Does the way in which Facebook works lead to disinhibited egotists telling what amounts to little more than outrageous porkies?

But most important of all is the problem of disclosure and privacy. To what extent can individuals prevent sensitive personal information being 'indiscriminately' spread? There are risks involved that people are becoming more aware of. And they are rightly worried, but often feel powerless.

Does Facebook make the socially rich even richer? Does it complement rather than replace the old, traditional, off-line, face-to-face communication? Or does it really help people whose friendship and business networks have been historically rather poor? Does it connect the disconnected and make the communication-poor rich instead? Alas not. The data show that the low self-esteem, highly anxious, high users do not make proportionately more friends.

So what is it to have a Facebook friend or a LinkedIn connection? It shows that you are alive, part of the new order, connected with (a form of) reality.

S. SPONSORSHIP

By their sponsorship shall ye know them. The corporate appetite for defining and stating their vision and value has not abated. And they can do it really well through sponsorship of people, events and the like.

Organizations seem not to be content with the simple assertion that the purpose is to *maximize shareholder returns*. Period. No, they want a feel-good, crypto-religious quest embodied in some creed.

So company 'values statements' are all about integrity, giving back to the community, being employer of choice, etc. This leads to a fun game for old cynics. Get together a dozen or so mission/value/vision statements and see if you can guess which organization they come from. That is, if you can see any fundamental difference between them. You can make it easier by turning it into a matching task: that is, you obtain the list of companies and a list of values and see if people can at least match them up. Piffle, twaddle and bull***t.

The moral of the story? You can learn very little about an organization – its profitability, what it's like to work for, its longevity – from the values statement. It seems to be there to make people in HR and PR, and even IR (Industrial Relations) feel better . . . but whether it has any beneficial effect on the brand is unsure.

Values, of course are *made manifest* in a number of ways. You can read company reports, hear the CEO speak, visit headquarters. There you get a better idea of the real organization.

There is another way of expressing values that really exercises the PR people. It is the idea of sponsorship, which has become something of a political issue. Consider the issues around fast food companies as Olympic sponsors. Sponsorship by tobacco companies has long been on the political agenda. Followed by booze companies. Now they are the usual targets of the protectionists – fizzy drinks, snacks, perhaps even toy companies. Activists brand them as the cause of everything from obesity to school failure.

But what of the issues for an organization not overburdened with a political agenda: sweatshops in the Far East, the destruction of the environment for raw materials; outsourcing to Third World countries.

Big companies are targeted by all sorts of people wanting sponsorship. Would you like to sponsor an endowed chair in a local university? Would you share the sponsorship for organizing a difficult and expensive sporting event? An expedition to Antarctica? A school playground? Food parcels to famine areas? The list is long and complex.

There are three big issues for those who decide on sponsorship. The first is the *match* or *fit* between the organization's products/processes/values and the sponsorship event/activity/purpose. Does it make sense in some way (e.g. a travel company sponsors some 'geographic interest' event)? Or is it symbolic? Why did Barclays sponsor Boris Bikes? Maybe the sponsorship could be compensatory. So food companies sponsor sport – burn up the calories you take in eating the product.

The second issue is *visibility/advertising*. Is it naïve to believe that sponsorship is a simple form of company altruism? Yes – it is really a subtle, perhaps rather powerful form of advertising. The sponsor wants acknowledgements. See how organizations such as museums, conferences and opera are getting better at all this – you can be a gold, silver or bronze sponsor. You can have your name written in that colour on a board in some prominent place. Or, even better, engraved in stone . . . for all time. It's a simple formula: More dosh, more exposure. You get a bigger logo. You get more seats for your clients.

This has become such big business that laws about corporate hospitality and bribery have recently been introduced. The 2010 act attempted to put a cap on all that wonderful corporate entertainment under the banner of sponsorship. It has been seen as little more than social bribery when the principle of reciprocity is turned on by cynical sponsors. We take you to an upmarket, celebrity event that we part-sponsor and in return you buy my product or keep using my services.

The third issue is *massed* vs *distributed* sponsorship. Should you just do one big thing and become known for it? You sponsor a new book prize (values: innovation, imagination, literature, creativity) or a big, perhaps minority, sporting event (values: fitness, determination, underdog). What about a building? That is serious dosh and lasts a long time.

Does putting all your eggs in one basket get a better payback than distributing the sponsorship money to a wider range of smaller activities. Muck spreading or cluster bombing? The trouble also with big sponsorship commitments is that they can tie you in for long periods of time. Indeed, too long. Changing fashions may mean today's sponsor target seriously loses its shine after a few years. In actual fact, it may turn out to be all rather embarrassing.

Big companies have to take sponsorship seriously, particularly if they are the major employer in a local area. Now the desire to be a 'good corporate citizen' is the driver. Sponsorship of local teams, crèches, youth and retirement clubs will touch many employees and the organization's image locally, even if the sponsorship is relatively small and never makes it to the national press.

Part IV

It's All in the Delivery – Management Behaviour

It is very easy for people to describe the characteristics of good and bad leaders they have encountered. Bad managers are often cold micro-managers, who care only about themselves. Good managers have integrity and courage. They also have political savvy and realize how important it is. Most importantly, they are able and willing to confront poor performance, which is a major source of demoralization and frustration in teams.

Great managers have the competence to do the job and the ability to inspire. They need to do so constantly and learn how to deal with difficult people, particularly those who disrupt teams. It is all about being insightful and persistent. And preventing problems escalating.

A. ALL THE QUESTIONS AND ALL THE ANSWERS

Fanatics and moderates are found as much in business as in religion and politics. By definition, fanatics are extremists. Some may be violent, many are militant and all are authoritarian. They have a distinctive mentality or a mindset. And it is one with clear answers, an agenda and always a righteous cause.

Since the war, psychologists have studied a wide array of extremist groups: anarchists, Bolsheviks, Fascists, Nazis and, more recently, Islamist militant extremists. One analysis of a couple of years ago identified a dozen or so features of the mindset of those with all the answers:

1. Perceived deprivation in relation to others.
2. A broad pervasive dissatisfaction with the world as it is.
3. A refusal to model themselves on some externally imposed idea of how one should behave.
4. A sense of being constantly and historically unfairly treated, with consequent feelings of injustice.
5. The feeling that no-one has a real say in decisions that affect them and that can help them escape their unfair situation.
6. An aggressive attitude and stance towards a very particular and identifiable enemy who is/was the real source of all their problems.
7. The simple sense of the end justifying the means in getting justice and restitution for oneself and one's group.
8. A clear us-vs-them, black-and-white, fall-or-be-killed style of thinking.
9. A strong belief that their cause is all that they are living for.
10. An obligation to follow all rules and conform to the behavioural norms of the group.
11. A serious conviction that 'heroic acts' will improve the world as a whole.
12. A utopian vision of a different, better world.

A more recent analysis by researchers in America, Central Europe and Singapore has identified various themes in the mindset of the militant extremist (*Perspectives on Psychological Science*, 2009). A useful checklist to detect possible terrorists at work? A way of predicting whether someone might prove to be a difficult trade-unionist.

The first theme is that difficult situations necessitate extreme, unconventional and unorthodox measures – read illegality, violence, brutality. The second is that clever trick of guilt-absolving, responsibility-denying gob-bledegook that makes their actions somehow morally defensible. Third, a lot of military terminology and dis-course – look for references to army, battlefield, armed struggle and War. Fourth, the clear belief that a group is being tragically and unjustly obstructed and denied its ability to attain its rightful position in the world.

Fifth, there is a simple, inaccurate view of history where there was a glorious, Golden Age – a period when they were 'top dog', the superior culture, and that they are inheritors of that magnificent tradition. Sixth, and related to the above, delusional utopianizing – a clear belief in the possibility of a new civilization, a harmoni-ous, everything paradise.

Seventh, an obsession with calamity, catastrophe and crisis – a way of portraying the present in alarmist terms. Eighth, and probably more associated with religious militants, the idea of *'deus ex machina'* – interventions of miracles and supernatural interventions, of hope from above. And ninth, in this tradition, the imperative to rid the world of evil – to purify the land and people so that it is cleansed of corruption.

Tenth, and perhaps most worrying, the glorification of martyrdom – of dying for the cause and being a just sacrifice for the glory of the cause.

Eleventh, that all good people have a duty and obligation to follow the dictates of the cause – namely to defend and to attack. There is a 'mustness' at work here – no choice, no ifs and buts. Twelfth is that old stalwart Machiavellianism 'in the service of the cause' – immoral means to immor-tal ends, force to achieve the goal.

Thirteenth, a curious desire to turn acceptable behav-iours and beliefs like bellicosity, intolerance and venge-ance into virtues. Children of an angry God despise cowardice, moderation and forgiveness. Fourteenth, a not uncommon trait of dehumanizing, demonizing and denouncing opponents as animals, devils or *untermensch*.

The last two beliefs are shared by many. One is the idea that the modern world – indeed, all aspects of modernity – is disastrous for humanity. Selfish, sinful, materialistic waste. But there is the more worrying view that the democratically elected civil government is actually illegitimate. The rulers, authorities and the elected have overstepped acceptable moral bounds and essentially forfeited their right to govern.

But is this militant-extremist fanatical thinking pattern utterly bizarre and essentially the beliefs of many people. Not at all. Some extreme environmentalists, animal rights activists and politicians hold the view. Believe you belong to a superior, vulnerable and helpless group that is unjustly treated – or that you speak on their behalf – and you have it in a nutshell.

B. BENEFITS OF ADVERSITY

Shit happens . . . the best-laid plans of mice and men and all that. The capriciousness of life means that, for nearly all of us, serious, sudden setbacks occur. Accidents, illness, the results of bad decisions. Wrong place, wrong time, wrong person, wrong idea.

This is all not so much a question of 'if' but 'when'. But the more important issue is how people react. Do setbacks strengthen or weaken people? Are they an all-important testing bed for the stresses of corporate life? Can they efficiently *inoculate* people against future disasters? Can they (ever) fulfil any useful function?

Or does it depend on the nature of the setback? Does it matter whose fault it was? Rather acute, or chronic? Can it be (for anyone) life threatening in the long term, regarding issues like post-traumatic stress disorder?

What if you were making a senior appointment and you knew that a candidate had lost his/her young spouse to cancer and was left with three young children? What if they had grown-up in a children's home because their parents could or would not look after them? What if they, unlike most others, had survived a traumatic accident? What if they had twice been made redundant from collapsing companies? Are you going to take this factor into consideration in your appointment?

Those interested in the psychology of loss (death, divorce, unemployment, emigration) note that there is a typical pattern. There are many interesting models, graphs and accounts, but it is always the story of a journey from shock and denial and anger through the dark night of the soul to acceptance and recovery. The length of the journey and the distress suffered on it vary widely.

Personal reactions to adversity vary in several ways. First, the very conception of what is a crisis, problem or nightmare differs enormously from one person to the next. That is, the same event is perceived very differently. One person's crisis is another's 'wake-up-call'. One person's slough of despondency is for another a time for serious reflection and realignment.

Second, people have characteristic and therefore predictable reactions to these events. They are called *preferred coping strategies*. Some are more successful than others. Some people take to their bed, others talk to their therapists, and others count their blessings. Clearly some are more successful than others. Third, though individuals may want to (and try to) change these reactions, these are pretty consistent over their lifetime.

There are different typical ways of reacting to setback. The first may be to deny, minimize or *suppress* the crisis. This can involve elaborate stories of extra-punitiveness, meaning that others are the cause and they bear the consequences. Or the reaction may take the form of serious stoicism. This is the Aussie male, Captain Scott approach, pretending that nothing serious has happened. Take it on the chin like a man. Don't complain.

This stoical approach is all about putting effort into the control of emotional expression and the attempt to conceal vulnerability of any kind. This unwillingness to seek (or indeed give) help can be perceived as cold and arrogant. And it is often linked to interpersonal difficulties.

The second type of reaction is the opposite. This is all about *catastrophization*. It's letting it all hang out, shrieking rather than crying for help. Turning molehills into mountains. Making it a crisis for all around.

Synonyms in psychology for 'neurotic' are 'unstable' or 'moody'. Neurotic individuals may not all experience great highs, but they do experience great lows. While their type of response to setbacks may be healthier than the stoical response, it can have many negative consequences. The crisis response is exhausting for others. These people tend to 'cry wolf' too often. They sap the energy of those around them, and over time they become isolated. So they cry all the more loudly and a negative cycle is established.

The third type of reaction is perhaps the best. It is rational, yet those individuals are not scared to express emotion. It's called *re-evaluation*. It can happen if you go to the funeral of a friend or family member. Suddenly, what is important in life seems a lot clearer. It's a time to realign the compass, to reset priorities, to clarify what matters.

Setbacks give feedback about what is important. They can be an opportunity, not a cost. This third type of reaction to setbacks is associated with resilience. Resilient people have a habit of positive reappraisal. They don't, of course, actively seek out setbacks, but they are less fazed by them. Some agree that mild setbacks actually help them. They test their supportive social network and increase their sense of coherence.

The paradox of high self-esteem and success is the sin of hubris. The great religions know about this. They keep their pastors poor so that they can empathize with others. There is nothing like seeing the spoilt, narcissistic brat, cushioned from all the hardships of life, fall off their perch screaming with indignation. There is an ugly side to a charmed life without adversity.

C. BUREAUCRATIC PUNISHMENT

See if you can identify with this story. Most managers in the organization do a *good enough* job. Some are outstanding. They set their staff challenging goals, help in their achievement, form and maintain high-performing teams, etc., etc. They understand and accept the duties that go with the rewards of leadership.

But some managers don't. They come in various forms and guises: the bully, the control freak, the loner and the absentee landlord. What they seem to have in common is that they don't give their staff much help, feedback or 'steer'. There may be many reasons why they can't or won't fulfil the basic requirements of management – techies not suited to people management, sub-clinical narcissists who think the job is really all about them, over-promoted, under-powered, second-raters. And the percentage of bad to good managers can and does have a long-term influence on the organization.

All very well, such is life. But what to do? You could try the Jack Welch 'surgical tithing' approach, where the bottom 10 per cent of managers are sacked each year. Sounds good if (and only if) they can be easily identified; the problem always lies with them; the process is seen as just. Not exactly the remedy for maintaining morale and engagement. Too much 'am I next?' paranoia. You also don't know what caused the problem in the first place – it is non-diagnostic ruthlessness.

So, step in traditional HR. The way to 'force' management to manage is to put in place a whole range of 'administrative' requirements. If managers won't give clear or reasonable directions/goals, they are required to specify not only their own but all their reports' *key*

performance indicators. And these are open to inspection
by senior managers and HR specialists to see if they fulfil
the *ordained structure* in the *required jargon* in the *right
format.*

Next, if they won't give feedback, they have to attend
regular one-on-one progress reviews and appraisals. And
there has to be paper proof of this. And this means all
the forms – lots of them – completed online, of course,
but no less onerous.

So begins the dreaded performance management
bureaucracy. The aim? Supposedly to promote good
management, provide equitable rewards and consistency across the organization. This means that it is not a
remedial process for those who are deemed 'not fulfilling
their management responsibilities' . . . but for everyone
beyond a certain level in the organization.

Yet what of the consequences? Remember the average
organization where most managers do a good (enough)
job. Suddenly, they are compelled to hold meetings, fill
out forms and the like. It may start out pretty informally
with reasonable flexibility and discretion. Nothing too
irksome for manager and staff member. Yet, by definition,
the weak managers resist all this stuff. So the whole thing
gets tightened up. The forms become longer, the threats
of non-compliance greater, the administrative burden
increased. Everyone is poked – increasingly easy with the
intranet. The ideal job for the passive-aggressive obses-
sional: to monitor, remind and basically annoy managers
into compliance with non-evidence-based requirements.

And the result? The good managers don't see the
point and resent the attempts to standardize, formalize
and bureaucratize the whole experience. They and their
staff were happy the way they did things previously – the
latter knew their targets, felt supported and got useful
feedback.

Worse, it has little beneficial effect on the bad managers, who still wriggle out of their fundamental supervisory

responsibilities. The ultimate law of unintended consequences: you alienate the competent ones while having little effect on those who don't deliver. Punish the able and ignore the troublemakers.

What about the staff of good and bad managers? Do they like being appraised in the formal way? Frequently, they do not. Soon a conspiracy culture grows. Managers, both good and bad, agree that the whole process misses the point. So they fill out the forms perfunctorily, cynically and resentfully. The good manager can feel as resentful as the bad one. As can the good employee. The good manager may feel their style is constrained, inhibited or directed. And the bad ones find ways around the whole process. The net result is less than satisfactory.

So, doctor, what to do? Start with the diagnosis. Why are some people poor managers? There are a number of explanations, but the most common is that they were promoted to management from the position of highly competent, technical, and task-oriented employee rewarded for performance. They weren't 'naturals' as managers even for their own people. So you have two options: hope that some sort of training works or give them fancy titles without managerial responsibility.

Next, rather than punish the ones doing a good job, reward them. Don't bureaucratize and formalize a natural process. Let them do it their way and make them examples of those who can inspire their staff.

But behind all this form-filling fetishism lies a growing monster that only feeds it: litigation and tribunals. The sour, vindictive worker who sues for being sacked uses their lack of proper appraisal and supervision as a (often very successful) plea.

D. CONSCIENTIOUSNESS

There is a day called Exaudi in the Christian callender, the Sunday after Ascension Day, which is the second most important occasion in the Church year (after Easter Day), commemorating the bodily ascension of Jesus into heaven.

It is significant for being an ecumenical feast (universally celebrated) and is a public holiday in at least 12 countries around the world, including, surprisingly, some strongly Protestant or secular states, such as Norway and the Netherlands. The French are famous for taking 'Le Pont' (bridge) between Ascension Day, which is always on a Thursday (40 days after Easter Sunday) and the weekend, effectively closing the country for two full working days.

Ascension Day is a holy day of obligation for Catholics, meaning the equivalent of a three-line whip for attendance at Mass. In some countries the obligation has been moved from Thursday to Sunday, making life easier where it is not a national holiday.

Yet how many Catholics will be conscientious enough to attend Mass on this significant day? Statistics show that weekly church attendance for Catholics in the UK is falling, as for Anglicans, and is projected to decline by a quarter over the next decade. In Ireland, the Archbishop of Dublin reported that in some Dublin parishes, Sunday Mass attendance is currently only 5 per cent of the Catholic population and in some cases as low as 2 per cent.

Does this suggest that people are becoming less conscientious? Is conscientiousness an outdated concept, as irrelevant to the modern world as the provision of sedan chair services? Or do the numbers represent a decline in faith? Those who are interested in the extrinsic nature of religion are very different from those interested in its intrinsic nature. For the former, Church is more of a social club and one Sunday is much like any other. For the intrinsics, Ascension Day is a great feast.

The concept of conscientiousness is in fact as relevant to the world of psychology and work as it has ever been. Conscientiousness has been found to be one of the 'Big Five' personality factors, along with extroversion, neuroticism, openness and agreeableness. It is one of the top two factors to predict occupational success. As Woody Allen said, 'The world belongs to those who show up.'

Conscientiousness is about being efficient, organized, reliable and responsible.

It is the trait of being painstaking and careful, or the quality of acting according to the dictates of one's conscience. It includes such elements as self-discipline, carefulness, thoroughness, organization, deliberation (the tendency to think carefully before acting) and the need for achievement.

Conscientious individuals are generally hardworking and reliable, and conscientiousness is a trait to be identified and sought in selection procedures. It is one of the best predictors of success at work for white- and blue-collar workers. The conscientious 'pitch up and pitch in'; they don't skive or cheat. They are, in short, *dependable*. They are not self-indulgent; they can postpone gratification. They set themselves high standards and strive to meet them.

Perhaps that is why academics seek out conscientious students, and managers seek out conscientious staff. It is important in both unskilled and highly skilled jobs. Ask a manager about the incidence of people phoning in sick and listen to their groans. Note how valuable conscientiousness is to them.

When taken to an extreme, very conscientious people may also become 'workaholics', perfectionists and compulsive in their behaviour. These people are not beneficial to the workplace. They have imbalanced lives, putting work before their relationships and obligations to their families. They seem to live to work, not work to live.

People who are low on conscientiousness are unreliable and irresponsible; they are lacking in self-discipline and are often quite unethical. They make poor workers, students and life partners. They are self-absorbed and usually unproductive. They always put themselves before the needs of others.

Professionalism is said to be defined as 'doing it when you don't feel like doing it'. Conscience is the motivator – it is a powerful force for good. Freudians call it the super-ego: that above the self.

And where does conscientiousness come from? Is there a gene waiting to be discovered that explains it all? Perhaps. But there is, as the Jesuits know, a time at which this trait can be trained, honed and developed. Give me a child until the age of seven . . . and all that.

A conscientious person has a conscience – that still, small voice that reminds one of right and wrong, of obligations to one's fellow man, of following the rules. Those without any conscience are psychopaths. No, not axe murderers from the shower scene in *Psycho* . . . if they are clever, good-looking and articulate, the City is an ideal playground; without such assets, they may have to become imposters, estate agents or dodgy preachers.

A conscience can slow you down. It can put a damp-ener on lots of potentially fun activities. But it is also one of the factors that get you out of a warm bed on a Sunday morning to spend a little time being thankful for what you have. And thankfulness is a positive, univer-sally expressed emotion, whether people subscribe to the Ascension Day belief or not.

E. DIFFICULT CONVERSATIONS

Most of us (have to) work in teams and this does not come easily for an individualistic culture that celebrates that wise old proverb 'Love many, trust few, and always paddle your own canoe.'

While we all have a powerful (biologically based) need to be part of a group (tribe, family, team) where we are valued, respected and understood, work teams, often unstable, don't fill that need.

Teams can be ineffective or downright dysfunctional. There are a number of indicators of poorly functioning teams. The first is around the aim, goal and purpose of the team's activities. Is everybody agreed and clear about where they are going and what they are trying to achieve? And why? Second, is there a lot of pretence of camaraderie, support and team spirit that is palpable nonsense? Third, do the people in the team help and support each other because they are (really) accountable to each other?

Perhaps the best index of the health of a team is its meetings. It is less about the frequency than the dynamics. Start with attendance. Who is always there and who practically never shows up? Which members usually arrive late and spend most of their time fiddling with their phone? Who speaks and who remains silent?

Another big issue is what is said or not said. Many groups can be extremely conflict averse. They soon develop 'group think' and ritualized behaviour to avoid ever discussing certain topics. The problem nearly always lies with 'big, strong, analytical chaps'. They can do good number tumbling, strategy implementations and process re-engineering, but they can't talk about their feelings. Worse, they can never reveal their vulnerabilities. It is seen as a sign of weakness to reveal doubts or disclose personal issues. It's partly about trust and partly about 'psychological mindedness'. This approach removes the personal from the business, the emotional from the rational, the doubt from the certainty. It's a 'don't go there' rule.

The trouble, as Robert Hogan so elegantly puts it, is that we have to get *along* with, but get *ahead* of people at the same time. Hence the pathology in the 'top team': the board. Most of them are in competition for the top job. Or they see everything, particularly the allocation of resources, in win-lose terms.

The leadership guru John Adair pointed out in his famous but simple 'Three Circles' model that working together involves focusing on three things: the individual, the team and the task. All are needy, and require attention and support. The problem is that most business people focus mainly on the task and occasionally on certain individuals (when they are playing up). No one seems to be responsible for, or know what to do with, the team. One-on-ones can be problematic, but a team discussion of how we behave towards one another is, for many, just too damn difficult. Best pretend it is nonsense and not necessary.

Over time, teams develop norms. It is said that teams go through various phases called 'forming', storming', 'norming' and 'performing'. It's about getting used to each other and finding a way of working together.

Some teams are simply nominal. Someone has ring-fenced a group of individuals and called them a team. They are given some insignia and told to work together, but they are still functionally independent.

Teams do develop strong norms: patterns of behaviour, strange etiquette. Where to sit, how to speak, when to meet. People take up roles: the leader, the joker, *'nyet'* (the naysayer), the strong, silent worker. Sometimes the participants are all very much alike and fight over playing the same part.

But perhaps the biggest issue is the ability of people to have *difficult conversations*. Can you really trust others and therefore say exactly what you think and feel?

Here are some of the subjects that cannot be talked about:

Uncertainty avoidance: Sometimes called intolerance of ambiguity. It means how comfortable people are with lack of clarity. All business is uncertain and unclear. But some like to pretend otherwise. They are made highly uncomfortable around estimates, projections, etc. Their need for certainty in a deeply uncertain world can be very problematic and lead to team conflict. Fear of the unknown is one of the most fundamental drivers of poor decision-making.

No admission of vulnerability: No emotions (of any sort) please. Do people express but cannot and will not talk about anger, envy, guilt or shame? Everything is discussed in terms of others – projected onto colleagues, clients, customers – but never the self. Some feel the more you reveal your vulnerability, the more likely you are to become a target.

Dealing with conflict: How to challenge each other, argue, disagree. This is about the passive-assertive-aggressive dimension. It is about how to stand up for your rights without becoming cold, passive or aggressive. There is much source of disagreement on in-groups. The question is: how to bring it into the open, to discuss openly and to resolve conflict.

Openness to change, coaching and development: Does or can the group deal with change? Can it even be positive about it? Do team members believe they can be coached, helped and assisted to be more adaptable, agile and agentic? Do they understand the drivers, and major forces of resistance to change?

Dealing with stress: Are the participants able to help one another, or do they move between fight and flight? Do they have their heads in the sand, the clouds, or their work, unable to stop thinking of themselves? Are they even prepared to admit they are stressed, anxious, even frightened?

The sign of a healthy team, then: Can and do they have (and resolve) difficult conversations on a regular basis?

F. FAMILY BUSINESS

It is very rare for a family business to survive four generations or more. Be it the local builder or the great landowner, the brilliant start-up entrepreneur or the colonial adventurer, it seems there are too many factors militating against companies successfully passing down the generations.

The same problems or issues probably beset everything that is passed down, from the ephemeral such as titles (without land) to copyrights. Somehow the offspring have rather different attitudes and abilities from their parents, despite their genetic inheritance.

Some professionals, such as lawyers, are surprised and disappointed that their children are very adamant about not following their parents, despite the fact there is an already established family tradition. They say they witnessed their parents' self-inflicted workaholism for 30 years, only for them to drop dead on the golf course at 62. Poor exchange given the slog.

Even in Asia, where there are hundreds of small family businesses, survival is difficult. Children don't aspire to the values or lifestyle of their parents. Times change, and the better-educated and more Westernized young people aspire to different things.

The Asians specialize in nepotism. Rather than see the practice of hiring and promoting your family members as sinful and worthy of rebuke, they do the opposite. And they can make a good case. First, your family shares your genes. You established and grew the company and (maybe) they have the ingredients to do likewise. Second, you (really do) know all about your family; no chance of them telling 'porkies' at interviews about their education, their hobbies and their motives. Third, you have (probably, usually) brought them up to share your values. You believe they are on the same page. Ideal hires then?

There is a serious academic interest in the longevity of family businesses. How to understand their particular dynamics, their distinct advantages and disadvantages?

There are perhaps three clear reasons why children do not follow the path of their parents. The *first* has been variously described vulgarly as 'throwback' or, more sophisticatedly, 'regression to the mean'. It means that the more 'extreme' individuals are in any dimension (charisma, intellect, creativity), the less likely it is their children will score so highly. That is, the offspring become more 'normal', less extreme, more average.

There is an excellent story to illustrate this point that was first told by a psychologist who won the Nobel Prize for economics. An Israeli conscript in the air force, he asked pilot instructors, who witnessed their pupils taking off and landing again and again, whether punishment or reward (stick or carrot) worked best. The instructors said that it depended. After a particularly good landing there was lots of fulsome hearty praise. Equally, after a bad landing, they gave some pretty direct, negative feedback, with niceties and sensitivities omitted. They then observed the effect: did praise sustain good performance and did criticism improve performance?

The instructors were very clear about what happened: praise did not work, but punishment did. But they were wrong! They had witnessed the simple regression to the mean phenomenon. Extreme success was followed by less success, and likewise with failure. The bad landing was almost always followed by a better one. So they believed punishment worked.

Regression to the mean happens. Off spring can be more like their grand- or even great-grand-parents than their parents. They seem less talented, less exceptional, less committed.

The second reason, which is equally important, is that the children are spoilt. The success and wealth of the parents leads them to giving their children the best of everything. And that means they become used to having a whole range of advantages. The best schooling, the newest toys, the most exotic holidays.

The 'from the gutter to the gutter in two generations' phenomenon is well known. We also know that scions of distinguished aristocrats fritter away their (vast) inheritances on traditional vices. Their psychologists sometimes call this 'the imposter syndrome': the idea that their titles, which they did not earn, makes people treat them differently (which they do not like). It means people may have expectations of them that they cannot or will not fulfil, so they 'throw it all away'.

It is interesting that some very rich and successful entrepreneurs try hard not to spoil their children. Some try to restrict their incomes, others leave all their money in complicated trusts demanding that certain conditions have to be fulfiled before they inherit a penny. This is often much more than turning 21 or 30. Rather it has to do with how they spend the money, on whom, and for what purpose – their contribution to society, rather than just themselves.

The third issue is the social constraints in family businesses. 'God gave us our friends and the devil our relations.' You choose, cultivate and drop friends. You change and so do they, and you move on. But this is much trickier with family members, some of whom may be free-loaders, scroungers or simply short-changed.

We know that rumination – the constant thoughts about work while at home – leads to stress. With a family business, you are often forever at work. Personal issues become business issues and vice versa.

All good reasons to stress the moral and rational problems of nepotism.

G. FEEDING NARCISSISM

Almost on a weekly basis now, I receive a letter, nearly always from America, from a rather grand-sounding organization. It states that an institute, committee, board or foundation has been considering my contribution to knowledge, science, society . . . and the universe. As a consequence of their long, thoughtful and evidence-based considerations I am to be awarded an order, certificate, mention in a very important book. After years of unrecognized devotion to my craft, I have at last been seen for what I really am: a hero.

I will be pleased to learn that my achievements have (at least) rightly been honoured. I am to be inducted into the *Order of Merit* or appear in the magnificent tome *Who's Who in 21st Century Science*. There are usually a few other offers provided in the well-produced, computer-generated letter. First, would I like a magnificent customized, gilt-lettered, oak plaque (see coloured example) which I can proudly display? This may come in two versions, depending on size and materials, and priced somewhat differently. Second, if I complete some deeply ethnocentrically American questionnaire, I will be mentioned in a vast leather-bound tome that lists all us 'heroes of the revolution'. This also comes in different versions. If I choose the top-of-the-range plaque and volume, I may be set back around £600.

There was an earlier elaboration of *Who's Who*. Suddenly there was 'Who's Who in Scunthorpe' or 'the South-West'. Then specialist versions of *Who's Who* appeared, such as the 'Who's Who of Estate Agents' or 'Small Business Owners'. They make terribly sad reading as the faces of clearly not-very-successful people stare out, as much with amazement as glee that they have been recognized.

The question is, of course, who falls for this tosh? Is there no limit to the fragile vanity of some people that they are prepared to fork out good post-tax, discretionary income to bolster their egos in this way? Clearly not – it is a thriving business and a very nice little earner. The business model: the market is buoyant and ever growing – namely the vain; barriers-to-entry – very few; competitors – numerous but highly focused; staff costs – minimal; mark-up on product – 500–800 per cent.

The psychological term for these customers is 'narcissistic'. Narcissism is defined as pervasive pattern of grandiosity (in fantasy or behaviour), lack of empathy, and hypersensitivity to the evaluation of others, beginning by early adulthood and present in a variety of contexts.

Narcissists are boastful, pretentious and self-aggrandizing, over-estimating their own abilities and accomplishments while simultaneously deflating others. They compare themselves favourably to famous, privileged people, believing their own discovery as one of them is long overdue. They are surprisingly secure in their beliefs that they are gifted and unique, and they have special requirements beyond the comprehension of ordinary people.

At work, narcissistic individuals have a grandiose sense of self-importance (e.g. they exaggerate their achievements and talents, and they expect to be recognized as superior without commensurate achievements). Inevitably, they believe they rightly deserve all sorts of markers of their specialness: bigger offices and salary, inflated job titles, a bigger budget dedicated to their needs, more support staff, and greater liberty to do as they wish.

Narcissists are super self-confident – they express considerable self-certainty. They are 'self-people' – self-asserting, self-possessed, self-aggrandizing, self-preoccupied, self-loving – and ultimately self-destructive. They really seem to believe in themselves – they are sure that they have been born lucky. At work they are outgoing, high energy, competitive and very 'political'.

They are unsupportive but demand support for themselves. All are unwilling to recognize or identify with the feelings and needs of others, both in and out of the work environments. They have desperately low emotional intelligence, although they are apparently unaware of this. Indeed, they may assume they have superior emotional intelligence. Curiously, they are often envious of others and believe that others are envious of them. In this sense they are deluded. They show arrogant, haughty behaviours or attitudes all the time and everywhere at work (and home).

Paradoxically, their self-esteem is fragile, needing to be bolstered by constant attention and admiration from others. They expect their demands to be met by special favourable treatment. In doing so, they often exploit others because they form relationships specifically designed to enhance their self-esteem. They lack empathy, being totally self-absorbed. They are also envious of others and begrudge them their success. They are well known for their arrogance and their disdainful, patronizing attitude. As managers their difficult-to-fulfil needs can lead them to have problematic social relationships and make poor decisions.

This has led to the distinction between vulnerable and grandiose narcissists. Both are poor at relationships, lack empathy and are self-indulgent. But the vulnerable ones are defensive, inhibited and insecure, unlike the self-assured, exhibitionistic, secure, grandiose variety. So, there is the sad little vulnerable adolescent-type narcissism and full-blown arrogant sod narcissism.

But is this a pathologizing, psychobabble analysis of something rather simple? Is the market for all this pay-for-your-own-worthless-award stuff no more than a little bit of bolstering your self-esteem . . . cheaper than plastic surgery, more long-lasting than a smart haircut? We all like compliments and it is no more than that.

H. GOOD ADVICE

Sadly, it was an urban myth that Bill Gates penned 'Some Rules Kids Won't Learn in School'. Charles J. Sykes wrote the list and it was so funny, honest and succinct that it spread like wildfire through the Web. Teachers carry copies in their wallets, parents quote it at dinner parties.

It starts with 'Rule 1: life is not fair – get used to it'. Other rules include: 'The world won't care about your self-esteem'; 'If you mess up it's not your parents' fault'; 'Life is not divided into semesters' and 'Be nice to nerds'.

It's the sort of thing most people itch to say to spoilt, egocentric adolescents with an aura of entitlement – entitlement to resources from their parents, teachers, employers and the state. It's meant to be a reality check for young people. And so prescient has it been, it is attributed to one of the richest and most successful self-made men in the world.

One wonders how the target – namely 'young people' – respond when they hear the rules. Are they amused or shocked? Do they need immediate counselling and do they go to some authority to complain, hoping to punish and humiliate someone who has been so cruel, prejudicial and wrong? Or do they ponder on the wisdom of the words?

So how about an equivalent list for the board or a group of general managers? A few home truths for those who have lost touch, lost the plot, sometimes lost the will? What about a list for all those self-indulgent, resource-squandering, Baby Boomers who have taken so much and given so little? What about those smug middle-managers with a nice copper-bottom-based pension, keeping their head down until retirement? And what about all those management gurus who so convincingly 'know' the keys to staff engagement, which predicts performance, which predicts profit, etc?

Picture the scene: 20–30 of the top managers of an international conglomerate, flown in for a three-day jolly. Wonderful venue, terrific nosh, excellent outings. It's the last day, and the founder of the company has been invited to give the keynote address. He is wise, enormously successful and known for speaking his mind. He ascends the platform. He reveals the secrets of his and others' success. There are a dozen things the managers need to know:

1. People are nice to you because you hold a position of power, not because of your personality or popularity. As you rise in an organization, you tend to lose touch

with what people really think. Some like and respect you, buy many don't. In fact, if they know anything about you at all, it is negative.

2. Loyalty is a two-way process. Demanding that others always show their loyalty to you, the brand, the mission, only works if you demonstrate loyalty to them – truly and consistently. Give as you wish to receive.

3. Everyone has a sell-by date and it is possible many of you are past yours. People may be too frightened to tell you that you may not have what it takes any more in this fast-changing, technological world. You may just be a little too slow, too rigid and too fixed in the past to hold down your current position.

4. Your PA is not your nanny, Miss Moneypenny or your personal rescuer. You should do adult-adult, not parent-child in your office and be able to manage your own agenda, calendar and schedule. And you should not have to be reminded to remember people's names, family circumstances and the like.

5. You probably don't deserve your salary. All that 'market forces for senior managers' malarkey is nonsense, and you know it. Best way to earn is to work smarter.

6. Don't be cocky when the results are good. It's easy to 'abolish boom and bust', as Gordon Brown said in a moment of hubris, only to blame some shadowy conspiracy of international bankers when the results were bad.

7. Mastering, publicizing and repeating your mission and values statement does little, except give the impression of hype and hypocrisy.

8. Measuring is not management. Target setting is easy. Helping people fulfil those targets is your real job.

9. You are in charge of your own development. And very expensive executive leadership courses at top business schools are mostly a waste of time.

10. Talk to your customers regularly. The one day a year on the complaints desk is not enough.
11. Pretending to be green does not work. It's often difficult, expensive and impractical to go green in the office. If you are not going to do it properly, keep your head down.
12. Be kind to your staff – it will probably be your only real legacy. Think of yourself as support staff.

The speaker will pause on the stage briefly, and sit down. For a few moments the managers will look at each other in disbelief as the old, comfortable shag pile of their familiar management styles is whisked from under their feet. A few may wonder whether the drinks were spiked at lunch. Then inevitably the stunned silence will turn into polite applause as the room remembers point number 1.

I. LIE DETECTORS

Usually, lying is hard work. Not the kind of white lies intended to avoid social embarrassment and injured feelings, but the serious lies with serious consequences. Claiming to do things you didn't do or to have been at an important event when really you were somewhere else. Lying is difficult and demanding because of things you have to do at the same time.

1. You have to get the 'story' right – it must be plausible and consistent with all known ('revealed' and revealable) facts.
2. You have to have memorized the story well so that you are completely consistent in retelling it many times and possibly being rewarded.
3. You have to scrutinize your interlocutors to ensure they are swallowing the bait.
4. Liars have to memorize the script but also perform – the emotions need to match the script. This takes effort.

5. As well as remembering the script, liars have to repress or suppress memories of the actual occurrence.

So it takes a good memory, acting skills, emotional intelligence and sheer effort to tell a lie (many times) convincingly and get away with it. That is why experts often talk of 'duping delight', which is essentially catching liars after the event by noticing how suddenly relieved and relaxed they have become since their performance ended.

Some experts in the area who published a study (*Current Directions in Psychological Science, Volume 20*) used this cognitive load. And it is because of the load that they recommend some pretty nifty tricks to catch liars. (Many of these are, of course, well known by the experts, who also know how difficult it is to catch liars by simply observing them because the cues are faint, subtle and unreliable.)

1. *Get the person to tell the story in reverse order*: It's not that easy to do but much easier if it has not been fabricated. Sequences are not always well thought through in the lied-about story and the fumbling-bumbling can soon be spotted.
2. *Does the person maintain eye contact in the telling?* Liars have to concentrate inwards and their gaze often shifts to motionless objects as they do this. Other people are arresting and distracting. Very difficult to maintain eye contact while trying to remember your lines.
3. *Ask the person questions they may not anticipate*: Liars are sensitive to having to say, 'I do not recall, remember, know.' It sounds fishy. So they learn to give plausible answers. So ask questions they don't expect more than once. If they lie about a meal, ask them what the other person ordered, who finished first, where their table was. Ask them about colours, smells, incidentals. Ask the same question again

phrased differently. Get them to draw a room and look for details.

4. *Devil's advocate*: A lot of lies are about opinions and beliefs. Good liars are usually able to articulate a clear ideological position. So ask them to be the devil's advocate – in fact, this amounts to giving their true opinions about an issue. They are faster and give richer, more complex answers than those who actually lied.

Strategic questioning

Most liars have to do avoidance and denial – they need a number of strategies to avoid admitting or describing truthful events, as well as denial strategies. Innocent people say more, fearing interviewers do not have all the facts; guilty people say less for fear of incrimination, etc. So clever people ask open and then closed questions. Innocent people are more likely to spontaneously offer facts, whereas liars do not.

The use of these and other specific techniques depends on the situation, the crime and the preferences for lie detectors. The trouble with lying is that to be successful you have to be skilful, determined and well prepared. It helps to have a weak conscience because you don't want to 'leak' too much in the setting.

The trick for the lie detector is to make it difficult for the liar to continue with the lie. You've got to be smart to outsmart the professional detectors. And learning how they do it may help the liar do it better.

J. LOSING YOUR MINDFULNESS

The Buddhists have always known about it. So have mystics and most other religions. Yoga and Tai Chi place it at the centre of their practice. Mindfulness means being aware and in the moment. Or, if you want a bit of psychobabble, a set of self-regulatory practices that focus on training attention and awareness to bring mental processes under greater voluntary control in order to foster general well-being.

It aims to 'harness attentional capacities which facilitate effective emotional regulation'. The aim of mindfulness is greater calmness, clarity and concentration. Much more than relaxation, it is about focus within and without.

The research on those who meditate (properly and with sustained effort) shows multiple benefits. They report more positive and fewer negative emotions. They also claim to have a better memory. And they can focus for longer periods on relevant issues. Meditators claim to feel more creative and flexible.

Mindfulness training can have interpersonal benefits: couples seem more aware of each other; bosses seem to be more observant of their staff, who, in turn, are more tuned in to their customers.

The list of potential benefits goes on from self-insights to mortality. What's that? Mindfulness makes you live longer? Well, possibly, because it makes you more aware – aware of what you are eating and drinking, how you are standing and sitting, what people are trying to communicate. It facilitates changing your behaviour. Makes you listen to your body. Are you really hungry? What exactly are they saying? What do you feel (deep down) right now?

Coaches, counsellors and therapists encourage mindfulness. It does, they claim, offer many benefits. Being sensitive and aware means more compassionate and empathic interactions. People who practice mindfulness feel others' pain better because they tune into their own. They have better counselling skills because they are more attentive to process.

And the list goes on. Mindfulness enhances emotional intelligence and social connectedness. The research is now backed up by 'real' scientists: the biological and neuropsychologists. Yes, mindfulness really can be measured by immunoreactivity and functional magnetic resonance imaging (FMRI) scanning. Stuff happens in the body.

You may be able to see on a screen that people are more patient, more aware, more intentional. For some, mindfulness training may be a highly cost-effective cure/intervention for burnout. People in the caring professions are pretty prone to mid- (even early) career emotional burnout. Rather than pills or expensive sabbaticals the 10-week (part-time) meditation course, might be 'just the ticket'.

But three questions remain. First, does investment in mindfulness training affect the bottom line? Does it translate to therapy outcome, customer satisfaction, sales success? Less evidence here and what we have is more equivocal. Meditation and mindfulness can encourage people to focus too much inward and not enough outward. It is a bit too 'me, me, me'. Shouldn't be, but it is. Too much analysis on how others affect me and not enough on how to deal with them. Good for the meditator; not sure how good for the business. The realistic, hard-headed manager wants some pretty good return on investment (ROI) data. Fair enough.

Second, does it last? Is it true that diets make you fat? The reasons are multiple but mainly because when they end we resume the lifestyle that made us fat in the first place. Only a change in lifestyle really works. Just as a puppy is not just for Christmas, so 10 weeks of meditation and mindfulness training is not the end. Mindfulness is a state you have to constantly work on – witness Buddhist monks and nuns.

It is all about teaching changes in awareness, emotional regulation and focus. It is about feeling, seeing and thinking differently. That has to be constantly worked on. The more different this 'way of being' is for an individual, the more work that needs to be done.

Third, what are the real enemies of mindfulness? Probably social media, most of the time. Bombarded by emails, texts, tweets and calls, the modern person seems to have little chance of being mindful. The paradox is that electronic other-connectedness limits real-life social connectedness. The recommendation: take an email vacation, give up your smartphone for Lent, consider tweets as treats – rare, slightly naughty indulgences.

Here the data may be worrying for managers and supervisors. A few studies have shown that workers who were allowed or even commanded to ignore all emails for a full working week felt better, had lower heart rates and were more productive. They said they could much more easily stay on task with fewer interruptions. They could concentrate.

The world is increasingly full of distractions. It is hard to be in a quiet place. The social media are addictive: an addiction that seems not only acceptable, but even compulsory. It is the enemy of mindfulness.

Good idea? All that Timothy Leary stuff about 'turn on, tune in, drop out'. Most staff are less stressed when encouraged to ignore their customers. But perhaps it is not that great if you are told that your advisor, coach, or therapist can't see you or speak to you now because they are on their 'mindfulness break'.

K. MANAGERIALLY UNEXPLAINED SYMPTOMS

Consider the following three problems

Hypochondriacs: Individuals with a morbid concern about their health and persistent, but unfounded, beliefs that they are suffering from (many, serious) physical diseases.

Cyberchondriacs: Individuals who use the Web for medical information leading them (falsely) to believe they are suffering from a (wide) range of (exotic and serious) illnesses.

HRchondriacs: Individuals sick to death of the petty, pointless piffle that HR insists upon.

The term 'medically unexplained symptoms' (MUS) is a (sort of) failed diagnosis. Patients report consistent, even debilitating, symptoms which cannot be explained by regular medical science. The cause is a mystery. The cure and treatment are therefore uncertain.

For some, MUS is not unlike LMF (low moral fibre), the most damning of all military diagnoses a generation ago. Is MUS too often malingering? Or a sign of neuroticism? Or will 'social science' show how people suffering from these conditions have been abused, misunderstood and inappropriately stereotyped.

The trouble with these labels is that not only can they be very misleading and also very unreliably used in diagnoses, but they don't suggest a treatment. In the workplace what a manager wants to know is *why* people are so frequently absent; *why* their customer feedback is so poor; *why* their productivity levels are so much lower than other people's. It is all the more important to senior managers.

There is an HR approach to all this. It is legalistic, procedural and well documented. You get the data, give a series of warnings . . . follow the rules, manage them out, don't lose any costly legalistic appeals.

The medical and psychological approach, however, starts with an attempt at diagnosis. It's followed by the application of a label that has meaning. So consider the following: A poorly performing person complains consistently about feeling both misunderstood and unappreciated. Alternating between sullen and argumentative, s/he is resentful of the more fortunate and hard-working. This type scorns and snipes at authority and shows passive resistance, alternating between defiance and contrition.

Recognize these people at work? Doing purposefully ineffective work, avoiding obligations by 'forgetting', obstructing others' efforts, resenting all suggestions for improvement. Petulant, brooding, negative.

What would you call/label them and what would you do? Call them a nuisance and sack them by any means possible? How about a little pathology, such as passive/aggressive (negativistic) personality disorder or dysphonic, hostile-externalizing types? They need counselling, therapy or medication.

For some, the bad, mad, sad trilogy is a useful start. Is the problem moral, psychological or genetic? Can the problem be fixed or not? And at what cost?

But there is an important earlier question to ask even before diagnosis and cure/treatment: what is the cause? Most organizations spend, quite wisely, considerable effort selecting the right people. They hope the bad, mad and sad are not selected in the first place.

So how do these people come to be like that? Is it possible that the way they are managed and supervised causes the problem? Young people rarely start out alienated, angry or disaffected.

Often the opposite – they are ambitious, energetic and forward-looking.

A problem soon arises if these ambitions are not managed. Who ever asks them about how, when and why people get promoted or get a pay increase? Are they clear about their objectives, targets and goals and what really good performance looks like? Maybe poor managers 'make' or cause good people to go bad, the healthy to get sick, the focused to lose their way?

Some organizations have 'sick cultures'. Just as there are 'sick families' that are the cause of childhood misery and pathology, so there are neurotic, paranoid and depressive companies. Normal people naturally react to sick places, and some end up sick as a consequence. They catch the bug. In following implicit or explicit directives, they become unwell.

So back to the problematic employees and how to diagnose and treat. Question 1: Were they always like this? Do others agree with this description? Is there general agreement about the symptoms? Question 2: Are there quite a few in our organization like this? Is this in any sense unusual and abnormal or quite common? Does this behavioural syndrome exist more in some parts of the organization than others? Question 3: Are we in any way responsible for their problem? Is this behaviour a reaction to our management/supervisory style and values? Are we effectively blaming others for our own faults? If the answer is sincerely no, then let's try:

Q: Does this person have enough native ability, capacity, horse power to do this job?
Q: Has this person been properly trained?
Q: Are there chronic or acute pressures on this person outside the workplace (sick relatives, money problems)?

The idea is to rule out other possibilities before getting to the bad, mad, sad labels. The next step is to be very clear about the 'symptoms' so that they are readily recognized. They need to be abnormal as well as problematic. Only then should one try the morally defective, psychologically sick or 'poor sod' trilogy. Just as a bad workman blames his tools, so a bad manager blames their staff.

L. THE MARSHMALLOW TEST

There are some very famous psychological experiments. Perhaps the most famous is that of Milgram who, in 1961, showed how nice, ordinary, civilized people would apply lethal electric shocks to helpless psychology experiment participants if they were ordered/instructed to do so. The book was about obedience to authority and how seemingly gullible and naïve (and wicked) we all potentially can be.

Another was the Zimbardo prison study a decade later, which showed how an equally nice group of clever, talented, charming postgraduate students would degrade, intimidate and abuse each other if randomly allotted the role of 'guard' (vs a prisoner) in a prison.

Now the media have brought another simple but significant experiment to public notice. This did not involve pain, death or even discomfort. It involved nothing more dramatic that children eating marshmallows or not.

In the 1970s an American psychologist called Walter Mischel played a simple game with 500 four-year-olds. He gave them a choice: eat one (delicious, tempting) marshmallow right away or wait for him to return in just 15 minutes and eat two marshmallows instead. Videos on how the children behaved are charmingly amusing, particularly those who are seen trying hard to fight their urges to gobble up the tempting treat. Some looked away the whole time; others fixated on the one available. Some 'held out' for a few minutes but quite quickly gave in to temptation.

It is possible to see the effect of parenting in some of them. All those parental messages 'Save it for later', 'Family hold back', 'Others first', all of which are attempts to control greed. It is the opposite of the so-called gravestone one-liner: 'His problem was that instant gratification did not come quickly enough.'

The test was about the importance of impulse control and emotional regulation, often called *postponement of gratification*. But why this modest study has attracted attention is that the children, now in their forties, have been followed up.

And yes, you guessed it. The postponers did better in life. They were richer and even thinner than their impatient peers. They had achieved more at school and university. And they were less likely to experience all the negative aspects of life: addiction, divorce, etc.

The question is what one concludes from this study – some findings being more acceptable than others. The *first* is the stability of personality over time. You don't change much. Personality and ability are observable at four years old and predict what you are like 20, 40, even 60 years later. Yes, trauma, training and therapy can change you a bit, but often only externally.

The reason why people don't change that much is not only down to their genetics and biology. Different people experience the same situation quite differently. Some are happy at school; others are disaffected; some are angry for the rest of their lives. People at work are the same.

Your personality influences how you experience the world. It also shapes your choices – experiences do happen to us; but the older we get, the more we have opportunities to choose our experiences. In that sense the existentialists are right: we choose discomfort, misery and unhappiness.

And we tend to evoke different reactions in others. Extroverts are invited out more than introverts. Ghastly bores aren't invited back to jolly dinner parties, but raconteurs are.

So conclusion number one is that personality endureth. But this does not mean you can't shape behaviour. Middle-class parents eager to teach 'good behaviour', start their offspring on a carefully planned journey to learn self-control.

The second lesson of the study is all about impulsivity and its dangers. Many psychological conditions are marked by impulsivity (literally acting on impulse, whim or caprice with little forethought, planning or consideration for the consequences). Impulsive people get into trouble. They have accidents, say things they don't mean, generally cause mayhem.

Because the opposite of impulsivity is in some sense procrastination, some psychologists have distinguished between functional and dysfunctional impulsivity.

Functional impulsivity is more about *carpe diem* than anything else. It's about dealing with stuff as it comes up. And some of that can be dealt with quickly. The dysfunctional impulsive is massively stimulus hungry. They need a constant 'fix' of stimulation. And there are many attractive stimulus rushes available, from a double-double expresso or a Red Bull, to various white powders ingested nasally. Some get a rush driving fast cars or parachuting. Illicit sex does lot for the impulsive as can breaking the law.

And this flags up the third learning point. The children were being filmed and some were then quizzed about their behaviour afterwards. And yes – just as in other similar experiments, there was evidence that some children told porky pies. Of course four-year-olds are not, like adults, experienced and sophisticated dissimulators. Yet it seems shocking that they can and do attempt to deceive at that age.

Perhaps that is why old-fashioned books on childrearing stress the role of honesty and impulse control so much. Together these two attributes are taken as signs of maturity, of being a civilized human being, a good citizen. Marshmallow anyone?

M. NARCISSISTIC MANAGER

Several versions of the myth of Narcissus survive. They are warnings about hubris and pride Narcissus was the son of Cephissus, the river god. By the time Narcissus was 16, everyone recognized his ravishing beauty, but he scorned all lovers – of both sexes – because of his pride. The goddess Nemesis answered this prayer by arranging that Narcissus would stop to drink at a spring on the heights of Mount Helicon. As he looked into the water he saw his own reflection and instantly fell in love with the image. He could not embrace his reflection in the pool. Unable to tear himself away he remained until he died of starvation. But no body remained – in its place was a flower.

Poets, painters and moralists have been intrigued with the myth, seeking to interpret its meaning. The Freudians found the myth beguiling and sought intrapsychic and psychopathological interpretations. There have also been various illuminating psychological accounts of famous plays such as Miller's (1949) *Death of a Salesman* being a prototypic tales of narcissism.

At the heart of the myth is the caution of misperception and self-love – the idea that inaccurate self-perceptions can lead to tragic and self-defeating consequences. There appears to be a moral, social and clinical debate about narcissism. The moral issue concerns the evil of hubris; the social issue the benefit or otherwise of modesty; the clinical debate is about the consequence of misperception.

Psychologists have also attempted to measure narcissism and to distinguish it from a form of 'high self-esteem'. It has various clear components: First, *exploitativeness and entitlement*: the complete belief that one is very good at and entitled to manipulate people for one's own end. Second, the belief that one is *extremely talented at leadership* and all authority roles. Third, all that *superiority and arrogance* arising from the belief in being a 'born leader' and quite simply better than others. Fourth, that adolescent *self-absorption and self-admiration*: the belief that one is special and worthy of adoration and respect.

The pathologically over-self-confident managers really believe in themselves and in their abilities. They have no doubt that they are unique and special and that there is a reason for their being on this planet. They expect others to treat them well at all times.

They are fierce competitors, they love getting to the top and they enjoy staying there. They have no trouble visualizing themselves as the hero, the star, the best in their role, or the most accomplished in their field. They have a keen awareness of their thoughts and feelings and their overall inner state of being. They are certainly good at accepting compliments, praise, and admiration gracefully and with self-possession. But they often have an emotional vulnerability to the negative feelings and assessments of others, which are deeply felt, although they may be handled with the narcissist's style of customary grace.

It should not be assumed that narcissism is necessarily a handicap in business. Indeed, the opposite may be true. If managers are articulate, educated and intelligent as well as good-looking, their narcissism may be seen to be acceptable.

On the bright side, narcissists can be good delegators, good team builders and good deliverers. They can be good mentors and genuinely help others. However, subordinates soon learn that things go wrong if they do not follow certain rules:

- Everyone must acknowledge who is boss and accept rank and hierarchical structure.
- They must be absolutely loyal and never complain, criticize or compete. They should never take the credit and must acknowledge that this success is primarily due to the narcissist's talent, direction or insights.
- They should not expect the narcissist to be very interested in their personality, concerns or ambitions but they must be very interested in the narcissist's issues.
- They have to be attentive, giving and always flattering. They need to be sensitive to the whims, needs and desires of the narcissistic manager without expecting reciprocity.
- Narcissistic managers can be mean, angry or petulant when crossed or slighted, and quickly express anger, so subordinates have to be careful when working with them.

■ They need to watch out that a narcissistic manager's self-preoccupation, need for approbation and grandiosity do not impede business judgement and decision-making.

The dark side of narcissistic managers is that they tend to have shallow, functional, uncommitted relationships. Because they are both needy and egocentric they tend not to make close, supportive friendship networks in the workplace. They can often feel empty and neglected as a result.

Narcissistic leaders may have short-term advantages but long-term disadvantages because their consistent and persistent efforts are aimed at enhancing their self-image, which leads to group clashes.

The question about narcissism is to what extent it helps managers climb the greasy pole in business but then later causes derailment. We all want and admire self-confident managers with high self-esteem – comfortable in their own skin, aware of their own strengths. But success can lead to admiration and a distortion in feedback. Successful managers, blessed by hard-working staff and a successful organization in a growth market, may erroneously come to believe that they alone are architects of their success. And this starts the process of delusions of grandeur that get them in the end.

N. PASSIVE AGGRESSIVENESS

We rejoice, every so often, that we have eradicated an illness once so widespread and so lethal that millions died. Equally, some illnesses, such as TB, that were once thought to be consigned to history have reappeared to haunt us again.

But mental illnesses are a bit different. The issue is always whether some behaviour pattern should be considered a mental illness worthy of treatment. Critics talk of over-pathologizing. They talk of 'psychiatric political control' and how repressive regimes have used psychiatry to lock up people in mental hospitals with often worse conditions than prisons. And not so long ago, when homosexuality was regarded as a mental illness. Of late, the critics have lamented the massive growth in mental disorders. So bolshy adolescents have 'oppositional defiant disorder' and badly behaved, impulsive people of all ages have attention deficit hyperactive disorder (ADHD). There has been a massive increase in pathologization. Over-excited psychiatrists, like zoologists and botanists in a virgin country, seek to find and label new disorders like the latter do species.

However, what is less reported are the disorders that disappear over time from the textbooks. They vanish for various reasons. First, when investigated, the 'disorders' did not seem very debilitating at all. In fact, the opposite. Thus 'hysterical personality disorder' quietly disappeared and those 'affected' were able to carry on happily seeking the attention of others.

Second, most common, the 'illness' proved too unreliable to diagnose. Faced with the same patient, psychiatrists could not agree. One thought he had X, another Y, a third both X and Y, and yet another that he was basically OK. A very serious issue indicating that the diagnostic criteria were too vague or that the essential nature of the problem had yet to be clearly identified.

A third reason is even more bizarre. This is that so many people appeared to have this disorder that it could no longer be considered abnormal. After all, normality is a statistical concept. This has been the fate of a personality disorder: one that people know of, and that has passed into everyday language.

It all started 60 years ago with the *American Psychiatric Association's* publication of their first great manual (guidebook, dictionary, encyclopaedia). One of the dozen or so personality disorders listed was the passive-aggressive disorder. Within this framework three related types were identified: *passive dependents*, who were clingy, helpless and constantly indecisive; *passive-aggressives*, who were inefficient, pouty, stubborn, prone to procrastination and very obstructive; *aggressives*, who were destructive, irritable and resentful. Sixteen years later passive and aggressive were combined into a single disorder.

So we had the *passive-aggressive* individual. You must know the type at work. Those 'doing their own thing' with the very conscious 'right to be me'. They are the 'it's not my responsibility', leisurely types. They snipe rather than confront, and mask their opposition to and rebellion against authority. They shirk responsibility and sabotage others. Brilliant at breaking team morale, they generate nothing but animosity among their co-workers.

The *passive-aggressive* person is a p***-in-the-a*** person, marching to the beat of their own drum, supremely confident in their abilities and work ethic, and cynical, often undermining the skills and talents of others. At work they do (mostly) what is expected of them but no more. All demands for anything more are seen as exploitative, discriminating and unfair. And they are never cowed by authority. They are a supervisory and managerial nightmare.

The list of symptoms grew: apparent forgetfulness, dawdling and intentional inefficiency.

But by the third edition of the manual the syndrome was dropped. The reason: it was thought of not as syndrome or disorder but as a specific behavioural response to a particular (work) situation. Yes, you got it. It was the bosses' fault. And so widespread it was no longer an illness. The argumentative, irritable, leisurely sulker was all your fault. Your management style and your unfair and unreasonable demands caused it!

By the fourth edition of the manual (DSM-IV) the syndrome was renamed '*negativistic*', but was appendicized rather than put in the main text. Many of the behavioural descriptions remained the same (such as resistance to routine tasks, complaints about being misunderstood, sullen argumentativeness, scorn of all those in authority, envy and resentment of the relatively fortunate, perpetual and exaggerated complaints of personal misfortune). And, of course, the alternating between hostility and contrition which was the hallmark and origin of the original term.

And so passive-aggressive disorder was dispensed to the diagnostic graveyard – taken off the books. It was too common to be odd and too much of a reaction to situations. So, it was thought, you might be a p***-a*** at work but not at home; in one job but not another.

There are those eager to resurrect it. All disorders are the result of genetic-environment interaction – the biological predispositions and the abusive environment. But some people do seem to be p***-a*** carriers. These individuals feel at all times and in all circumstances unappreciated; they are moody complainers; they undermine operations with contempt. And they are irresponsible.

So is the miserable, jobs-worth type a result of bad management? Possibly. Are they a massive headache for management? Definitely. Are they treatable by TLC, good PMS and the like? Maybe.

O. RISKY TYPES

Selectors seem too often to miss risk taking or risk tolerance off their list of competencies that they consult when choosing managers. There is all that stuff about team work and customer service and maybe about decision-making, but that is usually about style of decision-making rather than appetite for risk. All important decisions involve risk . . . as do all changes, which is the big issue for most companies.

And yet we know three important things about risk. First, people at either end of the continuum are bad

news: both the super wary and the carefree adventurer
have habits and attitudes which are not good at work.
The one seems paralyzed, the other feckless. Second,
while we can examine risk in various domains like the
ethical, financial, health and recreational risks that people take, it seems there is more consistency than inconsistency. That is, there are risk-averse and risk-embracing
types. We live as we drive as we manage. Third, attitude
to risk is clearly related to those classic three variables:
age, sex and class.

Business, like life, is risky. Indeed, as Nehru noted:
being too cautious is one of the most risky positions you
can take. We have to make calculated decisions on a daily
basis.

A group of British psychologists headed up by Geoff
Trickey at PCL have identified eight types based on their
risk tolerance. At the bottom are the cautious, pessimistic and vigilant *wary* types, who seem terrified of failure.
They don't like change and favour convention and tradi-
tions. They are wary of all change, all innovations and
anything new.

Next are the *prudent*, who value predictability and
continuity to things new and different. They are careful,
conventional and conservative in their outlook.

Another low-risk tolerance type is called *intense*. They
are generous and passionate, enthusiastic and involved
but very self-critical and so less comfortable with risk.

The average risk taker is called *deliberate*. They are
even tempered, self-assured and well prepared. Their
attitude to risk is governed more by the head than the
heart. They like things to be balanced, sensible and sys-
tematic. They are not unnerved by radical ideas and
proposals.

Then there is the *spontaneous* type, who is average
in their risk tolerance but tends to be more emotionally
reactive and expressive. People of the heart. They can be

excitable and prone to the ups and downs of high hopes and many disappointments.

The high-risk tolerant types fall into two categories. First, there is the *composed* type, who seems positive, resilient and has little difficulty staying 'on task'. They are usually not thought of as reckless and can keep their nerve when required to do so. But there is also the *carefree* type – a free thinker, valuing their autonomy and independence. They cope well in fast-moving situations and are stabilized by their clear sense of direction. They enjoy challenging the status quo and breaking new ground.

Finally, there is the very high-risk tolerance group: the *adventurous*. Positive, upbeat and cool, they can seem poorly organized, impulsive and excitement seeking. They believe and act as if fate favours the bold. And they are happy to boldly go where others dare not.

What do the data show? First, women are less risky and more cautious than men. There are many more wary types, far fewer adventurous types. Various explanations are possible: it may be evolutionary . . . man the hunter, woman the home maker. Or, if you prefer, little girls are taught to be more cautious and less 'show-off' risky for good reason. Maybe that is why dangerous sports and jobs are dominated by men.

Next, the Baby Boomers are more wary then Generation X or Y. Or is that simply age? In fact, the data show the retiring Baby Boomers are pretty spontaneous. Perhaps all those memories of Flower Power, Woodstock and changing the world are still with them.

And public vs private sector? Not that difficult to guess. Lots and lots in the public sector are classified as *deliberate*, which is average rather than risk tolerant. Very few are *carefree* and quite a lot are *prudent*. Private sector people are pretty well evenly spread. The answer no doubt lies in the precise jobs they do. The PCL team investigated four jobs. They found most IT professionals were either adventurous or carefree; most engineers were composed or deliberate; most recruiters were carefree; and most auditors were deliberate.

This follows the Attraction, Selection, Socialization, Attrition model which accounts for silos and people in various groups being so similar. Your abilities, attitudes and personality (as well as risk aversion) lead you to be *attracted* to certain jobs. Those who fit the profile are *selected*. Then one is trained (or *socialized*) to conform to the rules, and those who don't like it leave (attrition). So we end up working with people like us with similar tastes for risk. Hence there are those swash-buckling types who thrive in risk cultures and those who abhor the very idea.

So the old question: Born or made? Trainable or untrainable? Can you encourage the wary to take more risks and the adventurous to be more cautious? Probably . . . if the rewards are right and if the experience is a good one.

P. TO BE A GROWN-UP

Educators, employers and customers of young people know that some are (happily) grown-up, some will grow up, and it appears that (alas) some will never grow up. To be an adult means to be fully developed, mature and responsible.

There are *legal* definitions of being an adult. Old enough to commit adultery, old enough to watch adult movies. Old enough to vote, drive a car, go into your local, die for your country, etc. Interesting how the age criterion varies for these. There are *biological* definitions of adulthood. It's about developing secondary sexual characteristics. But there do not appear to be *psychological* definitions of adulthood.

But what does it mean to be fully adult? And why is it so attractive, indeed necessary at work? Maturity does not necessarily equate with adulthood. And precocious children can display many adult characteristics. So what are they and where do they come from? They can be summed up as follows:

Emotional regulation: The hormonal teenage years are marked by moodiness, temper tantrums, bursts (often unanticipated and violent) of strong (usually negative) emotions. It is about impulse control. To what extent this '*sturm und drand*' could or should be blamed on biological factors or the evolutionary demands of growing up is not clear. What is clear, however, is the unattractiveness of those with little or no impulse control. Hot, passionate, unpredictable: this leads to poor decision-making.

Life is full of pressures, set backs and disappointments. It's how you cope with triumph and disaster (those two imposters) that counts. Adults, like boy scouts, have to learn to smile and whistle under all difficulties. They need to be emotionally aware but also know how to manage their emotions. Phobia is fear of fear and is provoked by situations that cause great stress. One needs to confront and conquer these fears.

Some are blessed with a stable temperament and that helps a great deal. Others are afflicted by moody, unstable nervousness. Neuroticism is linked to anxiety, depression, hypochondriasis and the like. To be grown-up, neurotics need to learn good coping skills. They need to find ways to cope with all the vicissitudes of life and not to make themselves a burden on others.

Parents, schools and other institutions that prepare the young make provision for the poor emotional regulator. There are proscriptive and prescriptive behaviours designed to teach the skills of emotional regulation and management. Some learn well, others not.

So look for coping strategies and how young people deal with disappointment – look at ability to manage stress and anxiety. The road to adulthood requires some important acquisitions:

Independence: Grown-ups can be self-contained. They have the capacity to manage their time, their assets. They are able to take decisions and live with the consequences. They are not chronically dependent on others for financial support, for decisional support or, indeed, for emotional support.

At work we are usually neither dependent nor independent but interdependent. We have to learn to depend on others for certain things at certain times and have others depend on us. But we have to learn to make decisions and take full responsibility for their consequences. We have to learn whom and when and how to ask for help, and not to be helpless, worried or paralyzed by not receiving help from others.

Rebellious adolescents learn how to separate themselves from their parents. But not all do. And that may be the problem.

Empathy and altruism: People notice the highly egocentric, narcissistic, 'Me, Me, Me' generation who believe the world rotates around them. They alone are important; their needs come first. It is the function of teachers, parents and employers to find and nurture their strengths and make life easy for them.

As a result, they have little or no time for others. Some are happy to 'save the planet' and 'eradicate poverty' as long as it does not in any way directly affect their self-indulgent lifestyle.

Perhaps it is because they have experienced so few setbacks themselves that they have little sense of the misfortune of others. An adult who has some experience of the dark night of the soul can readily feel and understand the pain and distress of others.

Social intelligence: This is old-fashioned social skills, charm, the ability to read others. Emotional intelligence is really only about understanding and managing emotions. The person with social intelligence picks up cues and reads social situations. They are perceptive and flexible. They can read between the lines and know how to respond. They have a repertoire of different behaviours, which makes them adaptable.

Adults understand etiquette and the point of it: to facilitate social interaction. They know when 'yes' means 'no' and how to present themselves in all kinds of social situations. They pick up, process and perform well in all aspects of everyday life.

Self-structure: Adults know how to manage their own time and space. They can organize themselves before, at and after work. They connect consequences. They can structure their thoughts and requests. They can, like long-distance runners, balance their energy. They can prioritize. They know what they can't do, what they struggle to do and what they can do easily.

Consider how the students or scholars behave in their free period. Do they use this wisely or not? How do they interpret the word 'free' in this context?

Some people are drawn to institutional life, where all things are ordered: dress, eating time, shifts, etc. They often cope badly when they do not have a structure imposed by others. And, paradoxically, it is the obedient types who fare the worst because they are used to being told what to do all the time. And when not told what to do, they fall to pieces.

So look carefully at the (young) person in front of you. Is s/he a grown-up? Nearly there, or still has a long way to go? Being adult is better.

Q. TRANSLATOR TRANSGRESSIONS

Pity the court translator. Distrust the market research data. Ponder your Google translation.

Truly things are lost *and* gained in translation. Translators, particularly those in possession of that highly prized ability to translate simultaneously are often exceptional in many ways. They are often products of mixed-tongue marriages or of highly peripatetic parents, or unusually linguistically talented.

Simultaneous translators can be in high demand and highly paid, particularly if they have mastered two less common but commercially or diplomatically important languages: Norwegian into Arabic or Russian into Swahili.

To translate usually means to repeat an idea, expression, or sentence from one language to another. It can mean to move place, substance or form. So Archbishops translate Bishops from one See to another. You also translate to heaven, if there is such a place (other than a South Sea island beach).

The problems with translation are the issue of gist and comprehension. President A proposes an idea to General B at a public forum where two translators are present. It is very important and they speak quickly. The translator's job is to take the idiosyncratic, colloquial and diplomatic idiom of A to ensure B understands what s/he is saying. They try to deliver the gist of the message.

Translators like to get an indication that the message has not only been received loud and clear but also comprehended. Imagine the frustration of accurately, honestly and very literally translating a sentence only to see the recipient clearly puzzled. Has the recipient not understood? Was there a problem with the translation? Should one start again and rephrase the sentence? The same idea, thought or proposal can be phrased very differently.

Court translators have to be very well trained. Judges and lawyers ask planned, specific and direct questions. The job of the translator is clear. Render it in the other language *exactly*. But what if the client is from another culture with a very different educational background, and appears not to understand? And how do you cope with irony or the fact that language A (English) may have half a dozen words of subtly different meaning from language B, which has a quarter of that number. There are three no-no's for the court translator:

1. *To exemplify*: That is to give (one or more) examples of the phrase or idea to ensure that the meaning is understood. But how prototypical are the examples? To what extent do they, in fact, convey a very different picture from the one intended?

   A common problem is differences in the meaning of acts in different cultures: the gift, the joke, the greeting.

2. *To modify*: That is, to modify the sentence in terms of the adjectives or sentence structure. Modification can be by using a slightly different word (= concept) which captures the meaning for the translator. Are you lying, dissimulating or being economical with the truth? Words in different languages carry very different historical baggage. Was the uncle gay, homosexual or queer? Words are carriers of ideology and the sensitive translator may be tempted to modify ideas to make them more palatable.

3. *To simplify*: Imagine the well-constructed, multi-clausal, legal question. 'I put it to you, that, despite your sensory shortcomings and apparent emotional fragility at the time, you were quite able (if not willing) to identify in significant detail the facial physiognomy and demeanor of the accused.' Would there not be a temptation to say, 'Did you recognize the murderer?' The problem of simplification results from different levels of *articulacy* between the two interlocutors. It can be the difference between formal and informal language, between educated precision-speak and less-educated colloquialism.

So, to what extent is it the task of the translator to ensure that the message has come across, that the recipient has understood?

Watch one of those *border crossing* programmes and you see that in Australia and New Zealand the officials using a live translator over a speaker phone. Is this simply the result of economic forces? The translator at home, working on a call-by-call basis rather than hanging about at airports must make economic sense.

The vigilant, doubting immigration officer asks a question. The translator does the job. The accused looks angry, puzzled, guilty. Does s/he respond, at least in terms of eye contact, to the telephone (i.e. gazes at and pays exclusive attention to the voice of the translator) or to the immigration officer?

Perhaps seeing the non-verbal leakage of the accused makes it easier for the translator to avoid the sins of exemplify, modify and simplify? Not seeing how the recipient reacts may be an advantage.

And what of the sex of the translator and his/her accent? Does that matter? Do men speak differently from women? Sure do. So what does it sound like having 'man talk' coming from a diminutive woman? And then there is accent. What if the extremely competent translator has a strong accent – Mexican say, or West Indian? Does that make a difference?

But perhaps these problems will be solved by technology. Soon we will have software clever enough to do all this without any of the translator transgressions?

R. U-TURNS

Why are politicians and – to a lesser extent – CEOs, so terrified, indeed even phobic, about changing their minds? The papers call it a U-turn, and many can remember Mrs Thatcher's famous 'You turn if you want to. The lady's not for turning!' speech.

Listen to how often politicians scorn each other for U-turns, even if they believe the revised decision or pledge is the better one. 'Got it wrong first time eh? Not so smarty then.' Enoch Powell knew this when he said that 'thinking again means that activity most unthinkable for politicians – unsaying what has been said'.

To change your mind seems like a major crime. To admit that you perhaps are infallible, have made an error, did not have the full truth, etc. is a serious no-no.

This perhaps explains why politicians seem so scared of, and are therefore skilled at avoiding, giving specific answers. For them the deep humiliation of having to say, 'I was wrong in my prediction', or worse, 'Alas I cannot do as I promised', is simply too painful to endure. So journalists go on courses to learn how to 'pin politicians down', to get them to commit to a future set of behaviours. Politicians, on the other hand, are groomed into being evasive, to use grand words and gestures that, if examined microscopically, are simply hollow. Paxo vs the hapless Chloe Smith was a perfect example of the genre.

There is no shame, indeed much rejoicing, when sinners repent. All addicts are encouraged to do a behavioural U-turn. To change their lives literally around. To turn your back on a previously selfish, indulgent life is to be congratulated. Therapists encourage it. To reframe, re-analyze, recompute. Change is hard, but it is necessary. And repentance might be a fundamental part of it.

Scientists have few problems with letting go a cherished theory or explanation once new data come in. That is how science works. That is how progress is made. Out with the old ideas/models/methods and in with the new.

But this is certainly not true of our political masters. Despite the fact that Enoch Powell was probably right when he said, 'All political careers end in failure', few politicians admit they would do anything different if they could turn the clock back. They may seem bent on defending outmoded, discredited, even bizarre ideas and strategies. Few 'cross the floor' as they used to do – except, of course, to leave a sinking ship. The only way to leave room for manoeuvre is not to say anything specific at all.

Perhaps the explanation for this rather odd state of affairs lies in our cultural valuing of the principle of consistency. It certainly is a fact well known to salespeople.

In our culture we prefer, indeed require, that if people take a stand, 'go on record', or publicly and unambiguously make a promise, people want them to stick to it. Women talk of men with 'commitment phobia'. They know that people align their behaviour with their commitments, particularly if they are made actively, openly and voluntarily. Men, like politicians, value 'a certain amount of leeway', opportunities to change their mind and go down a very different path.

We know that if people make an active, explicit choice, they are then much more likely to follow with action. Consider the first questions a car-salesman in a showroom might ask: 'Is the safety of your family a priority for you?' And, 'If the price were right, would you buy a car today?' Difficult to say 'no' to either. Then, of course, they show you a model that won a safety award, at a special discount price.

Wise managers know from experience that if you can persuade an employee or customer to agree to follow some course of action in writing, they are much more likely to fulfil the commitment. After a discussion, they ask the late, error-prone, passive-aggressive employee to put in writing (an email) that you both agreed the rules about obeying deadlines, checking (and re-checking) figures and drafts, and adopting a more positive upbeat approach. If the email is written they are *more likely* to do it.

It is even better to get a written statement in public. Imagine saying that you had cc'd email your staff about your commitment to change. That seriously increases commitment.

The same applies to New Year resolutions and other ideas about change. Make them specific, post them on

Facebook. Fear of public failure and inconsistency drives you to do what you promised. This is one reason for the success of Weight Watchers® and other group programmes vs the solitary gym membership which remains unused. The lesson for the manager is this: Resist the threat and punishment route. And don't do rewards either, because the behaviour will cease as soon as the rewards reduce or end. Start by trying to find out what the employee values (e.g. team spirit, customer praise) and then describe how the behaviours you desire are consistent with those values. Get him/her to agree, and tell others at the next team meeting.

Not all cultures are as obsessed with consistency as us. Some Asian cultures appear to be able to hold incompatible beliefs and values at the same time with no difficulty. Religions seem pretty good at this, and perhaps we should take a leaf out of their book.

No, this is not an argument against analytic integrity, an excuse for flim-flam and lazy thinking. But it *is* an argument for accepting change. All managers say how much difficulty they have in bringing about organizational change that is 'the key to survival'. True, but maybe personal change is harder. But it is not that difficult to say, 'Yes, I was wrong. I have changed my mind.' *Mea culpa*. 'I too am fallible, but now, I believe, we are on the right path.'

S. UNDERCOVER BOSS

There is a TV series about CEOs visiting the front line: It's called *Undercover Boss*. You really only need watch one episode to get the plot. It's *A Christmas Carol* for the 21st century. Franchised around the world, the American version is the most watchable for feelgood *schmaltz* at its most prototypic.

Interestingly, it originated on Channel 4 in 2009 and has really caught on. One of those popular programmes, like *Dragons' Den,* that seem to catch the popular imagination and reflect the *zeitgeist.* And it's reassuringly repetitive; you are quite certain about what you are going to get.

The Boss of the organization appears; cue private jet, plush boardroom, person of action. It's all privilege, power and pomp. The Boss decides to visit the coal face. See how the little people are getting on. See if they understand the mission-vision thing. And how lucky they are to be working for Acme Widgets, renamed Digital Solutions.

Scene two is make-up. The Boss fears s/he will be recognized and therefore won't really be able to go undercover. So the dapper suit is replaced by the honest workman's sturdy gear. Further, they all get an Andy Warhol ill-fitting wig.

Scenes three to six. On the job. The strategic, cerebral, super-competent Boss is turned into the hopeless, helpless and hapless semi-skilled labourer. The various scenes are of him/her with different characters. They, of course, are salt-of-the-earth American (or whatever) style. It is important to include the minority person of colour. The struggling single mother helps. These are all supporting actors.

The scenes have to show the following according to the script. The Boss has to make the following discoveries:

- Even menial jobs are more difficult than they look.
- Menial manual work is more tiring than running strategy meetings.
- Customers are fickle, demanding and rude.
- The little people have to be pretty resilient.
- The pay and conditions are poor.
- They either don't know, or care about, company strategy, goals, etc.
- They have a pretty low opinion of top management.

The latter two require the Boss to express some strong emotions: surprise, pity, regret. Quite a few close-ups are required. At some point the distraught Boss may tear off his wig and reveal his/her real self, unable to contain his/her emotional state.

And so to the final scene. Our supporting cast of actors are all invited to a 'conference'. There is some cock-and-bull line about showing a new product or whatever. But this is the crucial bit. The power of redemption. Ebenezer Scrooge turns nice guy.

The Boss tells his/her story. The supporting actors are amazed and amused. The Boss hands out (serious) prizes. Best if both parties choke with emotion: see Oscar-awards syndrome. The Boss promises to do better: to listen more carefully, communicate more regularly, repeat the exercise.

And the rich can enter the kingdom of heaven. The first will not be the last. The work ethic mantra is repeated.

But consider the problems for the producer and director of this new fairytale. How to select a Boss with the required acting skills? More importantly, what story is told to the little people when a fully sophisticated camera crew that one cannot acknowledge (never look at the camera) follows this daft 'rookie in a wig' for days on end?

What of all the out-takes where the Boss finds the staff shirking their duties, nicking the stock, or telling the all-important customers exactly what they think about them? Furious customers, lackadaisical staff and unprofitable outfits don't really make good television.

The British version of this usually occurs when the PR department alerts the local paper to the 'experiment' where the boss works in a call centre, on the complaints desk, or the production line for a day or two to get a real understanding of operations. Few details and no weeping required, though a picture in a funny hat helps. Good PR, minimum cost.

Imagine seeing one of these programmes as a shareholder. How do you feel about the fact the Boss was so out-of-touch? Or that s/he seemed to endorse a generous pay increase without benchmarking the current situations?

Good generals, bishops and headteachers all know their staff well. They don't shut themselves off in the high-security executive suite. They go out and greet the troops, shoot the breeze, get a sense of the pulse of the organization.

Perhaps this is all a backlash against the ever-growing pay difference between frontline and board-level staff. There is a move in the country to reduce the multiples the top people are paid relative to the average earner in the organization. In the UK, a CEO's multiple of average pay has risen 69 times to 145 times in only 10 years.

Bosses who live in gated communities, who are driven to work and who dwell in the first-class lounge seldom have much contact with ordinary people. They become an alien species with different lifestyles, hopes and aspirations.

All the more need to meet with the staff on a regular basis. But no need for wigs and weeping.

PART V

Learning on the Job

The world of work is changing fast. Technological and legal changes can have an immediate and powerful effect on many organizations. To stay ahead of the game we all have to learn new skills. Successful managers and leaders know this – they understand that learning is a life-long activity. Rather than finding this threatening, they are often excited by the prospect. In that sense, going on a training course is seen more as a reward than a punishment.

Resilience and self-awareness go hand in hand. The resilient manager knows what skills s/he has and how to keep them well practised. Moreover, they know how and what they need to learn to do even better.

A. ASSESSMENT AT WORK

Many middle-managers suffer Assessment Fatigue. Their eyes glaze over at the mention of their MBTI or Occupational Personality Questionnaire (OPQ) score. They know all about their 360-degree feedback and some have even become experts on obscure (and rather dodgy) tests pushed by consultants who are very out-of-date.

Assessment of people at work is performed usually for three reasons: *selection, appraisal/promotion, development*. Note the difference between an assessment vs a development centre. In fact, as we all know, some organizations present the former under the guise of the latter. You can't develop unless and until you have been assessed; but the latter seems so much more threatening than the former.

The aim of assessment for *development* usually concerns self-awareness. The idea is to put people through their paces (read: psychological tests, daft simulations, odd games) so that they can receive feedback about their abilities, personality, motivation and performance.

Good stuff feedback. But what are you supposed to do with it? Some analysts argue that 'the cure' consists of bringing stuff (the mud at the bottom of the pool) into consciousness. That's it! Now you know why you hold such odd, maladaptive beliefs, why you have such dysfunctional relationships, why you repeat (again and again) such bizarre behaviours . . . now you can change them because you know where they come from and what they mean.

For some, this is a bit like telling an obese person that the cause of their problem is eating too much and exercising too little. Even telling them that they often eat when they are not hungry does not really help.

The real question is: what sort of adult reaches middle-age and middle-management without being self-aware? Surely enough, people (spouse, parents, teachers) have told you about your strengths and . . . *developmental opportunities*. Surely early stretching assignments have proven hugely developmental.

Or perhaps the shocking truth is that neither the things you do well nor the things you do badly are that developmental. Or the effort and investment to achieve small personal changes are not really worth it. Indeed, the word 'development' for the battle-scarred, tired and over-assessed middle-aged executive is likely to lead to dread rather than joy. Unless, of course, the development is to be assigned a trophy 'executive coach' with whom to enjoy expensive chats.

The second type of assessment is *appraisal*. Often driven by a deeply bureaucratic and deeply resented HR system, the aim should be to focus on a person's past performance to help make decisions about remuneration and promotion. But we all know the problems of appraisal systems: there is often little or no reliable data about a person's actual job performance; any rating exercise has more to do with the rater than the rate; the constraints on having a really useful assessment by anyone with the time or inclination to conduct it. It means that the end result is too often a box-ticking exercise.

This leaves assessment for *selection*: many of us are old hands at selection. Educational institutions, clubs, financial organizations all require some sort of assessment. Even adopting a rescue cat necessitates assessment.

For most assessors or assessees the task is to measure *something* – some entity, often described in the jargon as 'competencies'. So the assessment is designed to diagnose *how much* of something (e.g. customer focus, teamwork skills, integrity) a person has. There is often an unspecified cut-off point, but the general idea is the more, the better. Ultimately the aim is to come up with a metric, a profile, a description which specifies that the candidate is sufficiently competent to have the job.

All sounds a bit dull. The language of competency seems pedestrian.

The problem with the entity approach to selection or the incremental approach of development is that both miss the more fundamental point that assessment is really about predicting *outcomes,* not describing behaviours. Academics want students to do well in their studies, enjoy themselves, fit in and be a credit to the institution. So they measure intelligence, extroversion, neuroticism and conscientiousness.

The question is: Do the competencies predict anything? Do the recognized high flyers have a distinct profile? Where is the evidence? Surely the assessment should be made only if it is relevant to a specified outcome, such as leading a department successfully or developing a new product.

People who do well at work tend to share the same characteristics: ability, ambition, social skills. Ability without ambition is wasted; ambition without ability is dangerous.

In many ways the quest of the biodata people (biographical markers of business success) is a good model. Find successful people by a clear definition and see what factors marked them out from their less successful peers. A problem with this strictly empirical and disinterested method is that it can generate issues which are a tad sensitive. What if the best predictors are gender or religion or physique?

The moral of the story, however, is simple. The job of most selection and appraisal assessment is to provide information which predicts business outcomes. Otherwise, it may be seen as a perhaps interesting but pointless exercise to measure some competency which frankly predicts very little.

B. BANG FOR YOUR BUCK

It has been called *the great training robbery*. It refers to an old debate: why is so much spent on leadership training when there is so little evidence that it works? Estimates of costs vary. A recent survey suggested that American firms spend $60 billion on leadership training per annum. Probably enough to bail out a small European country.

But is that money well spent? Does anyone really care? Shareholders should. Is leadership training done because everyone does it? Will you appear to be old-fashioned, out-of-date, and naïve if you don't join in? Is it simply too depressing and politically incorrect to admit that you actually can't train people to be leaders? They have it or they don't. Not 'everything is possible' with 10,000 hours of serious practice. Perhaps the Olympics will have a lot to answer for.

Maybe it is important for organizations to conduct (expensive) leadership training to prove to their (very special and demanding) talent groups that they are super/mega/uber heroes . . . who may leave unless they are indulged and re-affirmed? Or possibly you have the punishment model, where people are sent on training courses to help prove to themselves they aren't up to it? Those fun, outdoor training camps run by retired military sadists work well for this purpose.

There is another issue: coachability. This is more than being competent and having a desire for change. Executive coaches speak of the amazing paradox that those who most need help often shun it, while those who need it least are happy volunteers. Are some people more coachable, trainable, teachable than others? And if they have not learnt the skills so far, perhaps this indicates something.

The questions about leadership training are threefold. First, do potential students really want to improve their performance? Forget how, where and when the training is done. The question is simple: do they see the ultimate goal as doing the job better for the advantage of the organization?

Second, are they open, and responsive, to critical feedback that helps them learn? The nature of leadership involves confronting some problematic shortcomings, strong and maladaptive preferences and quirky habits. Will they *really* listen to, and act upon, the advice of those trying to help them?

Third, are they prepared to put in and sustain the effort required to be different, better and up-skilled? It is a bit like weight-loss programmes and diets. Harder to keep the pounds off for any period of time than lose them in the first place. Can they sustain, indeed even enhance, the new beliefs and behaviours that have been learnt at Leadership Training camp?

In order for leadership training to be effective, you need to be able to answer 'yes' to all three questions.

If leadership is defined in terms of *forming, directing, motivating and maintaining high-performance teams that deliver measurable superior performance* you have to ask what the premise of the leadership training is. Study after show shows the same thing with regard to what people want from their leaders. People have little difficulty stipulating the essential characteristics of a good leader.

We know from large-scale studies, replicated in different countries, that people want three characteristics in their leader: honesty/integrity, intelligence/competence and inspiration/motivational charisma. Now, boys and girls, tell me how, whether and when you can *train* these.

Let us start with integrity and honesty: sadly lacking in those 30 or so American CEOs languishing in prison. Ever heard of a course called 'Learn to Be More Honest?' Sure, many business schools have 'Corporate Ethics and Social Responsibility' courses but that is not quite the same.

It is no wonder that we have seen the rapid rise in the corporate psychopath. See the book *Snakes in Suits* for many descriptions of the conscience-free person who climbs the greasy pole so well.

Integrity and honesty can't be taught. You can be taught how to fake, to say the right words, to pretend. Integrity is about moral development and courage. Honest people tell the truth when it is difficult to do so and when it would be much easier to hide under a smoke screen of PR, waffle and flim-flam.

The problem is that integrity does not help you climb up the corporate ladder much. Game playing does and that often involves trickery, deception and porky pies. Perhaps that is why integration is in such short supply at the top of organizations. Equally, it is why strong sanctions and good corporate governance are necessary to curb the appetites, whims and naughtiness of the integrity-lite CEO.

Next, intelligence/competence: if this can be taught, there seems to be a lamentable shortage of courses available. Where are 'Be Brighter', 'Pep Up Your IQ',

'Advanced Smarts for Leaders'? Yes, you can learn skills, but brighter people learn better. Yes, with effort you can acquire a new knowledge base.

Intelligence is about cognitive efficiency – speed and accuracy of processing. And, alas, by late adolescence you should know how much you have or haven't got.

And that leaves charisma, presence, chutzpah. No courses either, no magic spray. Easy to recognize, impossible to teach. The most desirable of all characteristics.

So a Great Train Robbery after all?

C. EDUCATION

What is the difference between education, vocational training, vocational education and management training? How would you react to seeing the CV of a senior executive for a very serious (and seriously remunerated) job if s/he had a first degree in art history, or classics or divinity? What if it were accountancy, journalism or photography? Or sports science?

The attack on the humanities continues apace. The economic argument seems to prevail. Why should the taxpayer sponsor years at university for a student to emerge effectively unable to payback the vast sums spent? So let them pay for themselves. You want to study ancient history, a dead language or moral philosophy? You pay. A lot and for a long time.

Is the arts student a typical directionless layabout, turning up with a hangover to four lectures a week, while the earnest chemist is seen every afternoon in a white coat in the smelly lab? Could you make a case for the value of an arts degree? Not exclusively in terms of the skills you learn, but the whole experience. The classicists are used to this debate. And, because it is usually only possible to study classics at the best schools and universities, it is easy to point to the many enormously successful and high-profile (read, rich and famous) people with classics degrees.

There appear to be three dimensions to all disciplines. The first is whether a 'real' or a bogus discipline is nearly always called 'something studies'. The second is whether it is an art or a science. The third is whether it is strictly vocational or not. And these in certain people's views (dare they be called 'snobs') form a hierarchy of acceptable qualifications.

So at the top of the tree are the real disciplines that are not narrowly applied: physics, maths. And at the bottom, are the bogus, arty-farty, narrowly applied ones: event management, tourism studies.

Of course, there may be other criteria as well. These include the institution. Oxbridge, red brick, sixties, ex-poly to ex-nothing. Better a diploma in oriental anthropology from Oxbridge than a BSc in homeopathy from the University of the Watford Gap. Or what about the odd disciplines only found in foreign countries? How do you rate a PhD in realty (real estate) from Flyover State University, or a Masters in Marxism–Leninism from the Technical University of Stalingrad?

But what does it say to you if a person chose education over vocation. The equally talented, verbally agile, curious student who chose history over law, pure maths over actuarial science. Is the pursuit of knowledge for its own sake a pointless activity? Imagine reading film studies. The lazy person's literature degree? Amusing at dinner parties? A good – or perhaps overwhelming – companion at the Odeon, but hardly an asset in the boardroom?

For some, the acquisition of knowledge or skill must be explicit, purposeful, meaningful. It is an investment; a cost, with necessary payback. Too bad if others consider you to be a philistine. At least you can easily find a job.

The purpose of education is understanding. It is not directly to make people happy, healthy or rich. It may or may not have that effect.

Tosh, say many parents, politicians and pundits. Education must be focused. Like training. Specific skills, specific syllabus. Something useful. If it is not directly useful – read, has some cost-benefit analysis – it is either pointless or an expensive indulgence we cannot afford.

Some commercial organizations go so far as to instigate their own university- taught and awarded qualification, particularly the hallowed MBA. So, how about MBAs for BA, BT or BP from a serious business school? How are they different? How are they limited and specific to a particular discipline?

What some companies argue is this: It is good for our employees to acquire a qualification such as an MBA. It is very expensive but it is also very motivating for staff. They work harder to be selected for the course. The good ones stay longer. And, as a function of the education, they become better managers. But, we need to make it relevant to, and tailored for, our needs! So BP may need a whole course on the issues confronting the oil and gas industry, while the BA Students need more on challenges in the aviation industry, in addition to perhaps more on soft skills.

Most business schools have core and elective courses: the first compulsory and the latter voluntary. But some companies want to do the choosing. For the old-fashioned, education is about critical thinking. It is about finding and evaluating information. It is about the ability 'to understand the cause of things', which is the motto of the London School of Economics (LSE). It is about learning to think; and often about communicating in the spoken or the written word. And it may also concern the ability to retain – memorize – information.

Could one not expect a student of architecture or fine art to be knowledgeable and critical? To have specialist technical skills and knowledge, but also the ability to give a presentation, write a report, marshal an argument?

True, the arts graduate may be more comfortable with words and the science student better with numbers. But, as was observed by C. P. Snow over 60 years ago, the two cultures do not differ in ability or contribution.

Perhaps there is a pendulum swinging from over- to undervaluing vocational training. The first signal was sent when the proud polytechnics became second-rate universities. The next was to try to turn all nurses into graduates. It seemed that strictly vocational training was not thought of as having much inherent value. But now the pendulum is swinging back.

D. ELITE PERFORMERS

Most of us would love to be thought of as elite performers, top of the class, really talented. Such people surely are the most sought after at work. The simply gifted, those who apparently effortlessly bring home the golden prizes. Top of the tree.

To be part of an elite anything takes masses of effort, training and determination. It's often easier to describe an elite performer than understand how they became so good. They seem to see patterns differently, to read situations faster, to have a bigger repertoire of options, to be more confident and in control. It all looks so effortless, but that is not the case.

Studies of elite performers in the arts, sport and sciences have thrown up some really interesting findings. First, there is the 10-year rule. As a rule of thumb, it takes 10 years of intensive, focused 'full-on' training and practice to get there. That is a decade: that is dedication. Study the lives of top athletes, academics and musicians and you will see how true that is.

Second, elite performers seem to know about how to maximize practice. They may do as little as 4–5 hours per day – they break this into no more than hour-long sessions and they often have little naps between them. It's what the creativity researchers call 'incubation'. Work hard, but rest and let it all seep in.

Third, these people challenge themselves. They make it difficult for themselves. They prefer not to automate responses. They try out new ways of doing things. As a result, in practice – but in practice only – they often look less skilled and polished than less talented performers. They experiment and they set themselves tough, but attainable targets.

Thus, by these calculations, a performance that lasts 30 minutes to an hour takes the elite athlete or musician 20,000 hours of practice. That is a serious investment. That is the real commitment involved.

For how long and how enthusiastically people practice a skill and knowledge acquisition is crucial. One has to *invest* – seriously invest – time and expertise for the sake of one's art or sport or discipline. And this inevitably involves eschewing other, often very attractive activities. In this sense, some – but by no means all – elite performers seem a little narrow, even a little naïve. When others party, go on holiday or attend leisure events, the aspirant elite practises. They have to have iron discipline and a very real desire to 'win' to get there.

And most know there is a window in their lives where things are possible. It may have to do with physical fitness, energy or even financial constraints. Life, they know, is not a dress rehearsal.

But is that all? What about talent, abilities and genes? Training *unlocks* the genes; practice helps biology become destiny. Many people with prodigious talent seem to ignore it, downplay it or simply fail to exploit it. They happily adopt that, oh so British, self-deprecation policy that both disarms and perplexes foreigners. Further, this is also never understood by many contestants on those ubiquitous talent shows.

The training required to be an elite performer in any field is exceptionally demanding. It all looks very easy. It is patently not.

So, elite performers need a good start in life in two ways: their genetics and their parents, which are closely linked. They also need the sheer drive to succeed. This drive is their investment to do the training. It is the practice which is pretty key. It is how, for how long and to what end performers practise that really unlocks the genetic endowment and background advantages.

To look at talented and elite performers we forget the following:

1. How much they have to, do and will practise.
2. What they have sacrificed for the skill.
3. How they set their own targets.
4. How driven they have had to be.
5. How little they believe in chance, luck and personal gifts.

This is clearly not the message that one gets from self-help or management books, nor from the movies. They make it all rather simple, almost effortless. And that is seriously misleading, as can be found from most honest(ish) autobiographies.

There is also the issue of dealing with setbacks. One has, in any competitive area, to learn how to deal with a range of problems: stage fright, physical injury, being beaten by brilliant opponents. These experiences toughen up the elite performer but break the less well-adjusted one. There is nothing like adversity to focus drive and determination.

Students of the magical MBA or the part-time degree know the sacrifice that is involved there. If there are 24 hours in a day and you sleep for a third, how much of the remainder do you give to your friends/family and work.

The mastery of any skills comes easier to the talented, but all skills take practice. This includes all those skills one goes on training courses to achieve: presentational skills, negotiation skills, counselling skills and selling skills.

Remember the riposte to the question: how do you get to the Albert Hall or the Olympic stadium? The answer is not geographical; it is: 'Practice, practice, practice.'

E. HONEST EVALUATION

They certainly don't do it as they used to. A retired colleague with more than a touch of obsessive compulsive disorder (OCD) passed me a folder, given my interest in selection. It was the departmental guide to candidate selection in 1965. It is called *A Short Guide to the Use of Summary Scales*. It was meant to help academic staff, who always interviewed in pairs (to improve reliability), understand what the rating scale numbers meant.

I know the author well. An Austrian refugee from the Nazis, he arrived in this country, aged 13, and received a first-class degree from Oxford eight years later. He is a product of that age: erudite, well read but with a touch of insubordination. He belonged to the 'tell it as it is' school but with a hint of flourish.

The document is a guide to using the six rating scales that were required to be completed by the interviewers after the interview. There were six scales plus the recommendation. In addition, you were invited to add comments and to specify not only the time but the duration of the interview. All pretty standard stuff. The difference lies in the descriptions of the behaviours you might see.

What makes this interesting is that selectors did not simply rate the candidate on a seven-point, good–bad, high–low, select–reject scale, but that each of the seven points were behaviourally described – it is not always an easy task making clear but fine distinctions. Some believe they increase reliability.

The joy in this document is the forthright description of the low scores. Each section has a preamble. I can hear strongly the voice of the author. Thus, when assessing intellectual ability the rater is encouraged to consider environmental factors (home/school), not only the mark. And to rate some aspects of intelligence more than others. 'A flair for mathematics', for example, is likely to be of more academic value than the ability to provide a plausible, rational claim for not doing well at school. For *intellectual ability*, the second lowest score (2) read 'Hopelessly ill-equipped to deal with the requirements of the course' and a (1) was simply 'Decorticated preparation'.

Work habits is the second criterion. In the preamble (a paragraph or two) before the rating it is noted that some students may exhibit 'sheer idleness' while often simply having an 'inability' to manage their time. The lowest score is described thus: 'Likely to find real difficulty in settling down to consistent work, with unsound working habits so that when he works he can only do so at considerable cost to his general stability'.

The third rating is *motivation*, where the selector is advised to discover to what extent a candidate independently seeks outlets for his mental and other energies, and the degree of enthusiasm with which these activities are pursued. The second lowest score (2) is described as: 'Passive, indolent, unenthusiastic, looking for the easy way out. Unlikely to muster sufficient energy to meet course requirements'. But (1) is better still: 'Comatose. Mystery where candidate found energy to attend for interview'.

All psychologists know that the unstable (neurotic, narcissistic, nutters) are attracted to psychology as a discipline, perhaps in the vain hope of a cure. The fourth rating was for *emotional stability*. Hence the need to assess for adjustment or, as the Americans call it, 'negative affectivity'. There are five preamble paragraphs to guide the selector. These contain some wonderful pieces of advice. For example: 'The ability to adjust oneself to the environment is often of less value than the ability to adjust the environment to oneself'. The selector is warned about the possibility of the psychopath and is then given this advice: 'The neurotic with levels of aspiration, dependency or sex problems is less of a menace socially speaking'.

The top mark goes to: 'Steady as a rock, no risk, could sustain a series of traumata, or a steady, relentless emotional pressure without turning a hair'. And the lowest score is for: 'Psychotic or otherwise grossly disturbed. Urgently in need of treatment'.

Fifth is *social skills*. The interviewer is warned to look out for: 'Personality defects such as negativism, poorly controlled aggression, or other socially destructive tendencies which can exercise a corrosive influence throughout any social group. A sharp eye is needed if we wish to avoid lumbering the department with the kind of person who survives by making life intolerable for others'. The second lowest score reads: 'Serious disabilities. Likely to prove a disruptive influence', while the lowest score is pretty clear: 'A menace. Guaranteed to destroy the social fabric of any group'.

After the recommendation the interviewer is encouraged to write comments and 'to refine and amplify the rather crude and brutal indices of the rating scales. Oddities may be noted, reasons given, significant aspects emphasized, attention drawn to hidden qualities or defects and clinical hunches expounded'.

A revised version a year later adds the dimension of *social responsibility*. To get a score of (3) the candidate should show: 'Apathetic to needs of others, primary purpose to look after No 1', while the lower mark of (2) reads: 'Egotism blinds to needs of others, which are seldom recognized; a social parasite'.

How are they different today? The scales representing the criteria of interest are much the same. It is much easier to have a high–low rather than a behaviourally anchored scale. Imagine a troublesome, difficult, devious and rejected candidate passing on the rating to a tabloid newspaper after he or she had been labelled comatose, psychotic, indolent or a menace. Indeed, the act of doing this would prove that the rating was correct, but imagine what the consequences might be for all involved.

F. NARRATIVE SKILLS

Courses aimed at improving your presentation skills work on a very simple formula. It's called the 'before and after' proof. Soon after arriving you are required to give a short presentation. This is recorded. Almost by definition it is awful. After all, that is why you are on the course in the first place.

Faltering, anxiety destroyed, hopeless, hapless, helpless delegates stammer their way through five minutes of hell. Everyone is embarrassed. You recall little of what anyone said, partly because it was too fast or incoherent, but also because you could hardly take your eyes off all their neurotic twitching, fidgeting and sweating.

But by the end of the programme confidence has been built up and the final presentation is a marked improvement. It too is recorded. This is proof the course works. This is the trophy given to the students. You did it – you can do public speaking.

Attendees are told some interesting pointers about body language, and about PowerPoint slides. They might be taught about the 'Three Ps': Pitch, Pause and Pace. And they leave on a high – I can do it. Might even become a motivational speaker.

And yet, if you ask the delegates if they have ever been on such a course before, you may be surprised. For some it may be their third or sixth. So did the others not work? Are they here for a top-up? Did the magic wear off?

Many presentation-skills trainers realize that it is 'mainly about nerves'. They have read that the most common phobia in the world is public speaking. To have everybody's eyes trained on you. We have all experienced the dry mouth, beating heart, shaking hand bit. Overwhelmed with anxiety.

The implicit idea for many trainers is to reduce anxiety by increasing self-confidence. This, they believe, will in turn improve performance. Well, half true. It is a bit like the now discredited self-esteem philosophy that feeds a fragile narcissism in young people. All that the emphasis on self-esteem did was fuel a narcissism epidemic, with little effect on their skills or learning. Coaches, therapists and trainers certainly know the importance of self-awareness. There is *trait* self-awareness, which is being aware of your personality trait preferences. For instance, extroverts seek social stimulation while introverts try to avoid it.

But equally important is *state* self-awareness: how are you feeling right now? It is about body mindfulness. Concentrating on emotions manifest in breathing, heart-rate, sweating, etc. Yet more relevant and important is how to change the state, particularly if it is associated with panic or stress. How, in short, to relax. Deep breathing, slower pace, etc.

You don't want to be too relaxed. Enoch Powell famously gave his speeches with a slightly uncomfortable full bladder. It seemed to fuel his passion, if not his urgency. Actors have to learn how to become tearful on stage. They employ a variety of mood-changing techniques.

But emotional regulation is only half the story. Some epic bores are, and always have been, calm, if not excited, when public speaking, preaching, or eulogizing. The question is: what else do you need to be a great speaker? Yes, we know about pregnant pauses, sweeping the audience with your gaze, smiling (where appropriate), the importance of 'holding' or maintaining gestures. But what of content? How to make it memorable? How to hold the audience in your hand? What are the secrets of impactfulness? It helps to study great speeches – often surprisingly short ones, such as the 'Gettysburg Address' or Churchill's wartime radio broadcasts.

Gurus in the area stress the importance of repetition: 'I have a dream', 'Yes, we can!' The importance of having three examples of things at a time, the importance of contrasts.

But some have forgotten the very simple truth of *narrative*. We remember stories. Call them 'case studies' or parables. They are, and have been, for centuries the best way of passing on messages, even wisdom. Yes, we also know about structure – beginning, middle, end – and the power of surprise.

One less well-known but crucially important feature of good speeches comes from emotion science. We are, it seems, more sensitive to, more successful at retaining and more attentive to stories with emotion. And personalizing the story really helps. That is why charities love a 'banner boy or girl' for their cause. Stephen Fry for bipolar, Bob Monkhouse for prostate cancer. Tell your story straight – with the pain and embarrassment – and people really do remember.

Note how the television camera pans in to any speaker at the first sign of tearfulness or choking up. The smallest sign of emotion becomes headline news – Mandelson wiping away a tear when talking about his father or Ed Balls on the *Antique Roadshow*. Emotions seem more honest than smiles.

For good advice, listen to *This Week's Appeal*. The speaker has one go and less than five minutes. The results are measureable: dosh received. And the formula? Best is a celebrity with a recognizable voice: get them to tell a simple touching story of a recipient of the appeal funds and how it radically changed their lives. Tweak heart strings to release purse strings. Focus on a range of emotions. Don't overload with facts. Picture the listener at home. Get their attention, make the message memorable, make donation easy. And, if at all possible, find a celebrity with a personal story.

You have to be skilful with emotion. Enough, not too much. It must not take away from the focus of the message. But it must underline it.

So, to be a highly successful, persuasive, and even well-paid public speaker, don't be too obsessed by PowerPoint and getting all the facts right. Learn to tell stories with and about emotions. Don't fear repetition. Aim at the hearts of the audience. That will inform the head.

G. WHATEVER HAPPENED TO HUMILITY?

Some experts claim there is an epidemic of narcissism. Arrogant, hubristic, haughty young people are the norm. The sneering, supercilious student; the egotistical, selfish, dismissive intern; the pompous, attention-seeking and compliment-demanding executive.

The narcissism disease was probably both started and spread by the self-esteem movement that inevitably began in America. Teachers worried about (mostly minority) students who did badly at school. They noticed that their bad results led them to feel bad about themselves and rebel.

They argued, with more passion than evidence, that the way to get them to do better at school was to work on their self-esteem more than their maths or grammar. The naïve belief took off that if you felt better about yourself, you could release, discover and celebrate your natural abilities.

This madness was fuelled by the 'multiple intelligence' gurus who were happy to put the word 'intelligence' after any human capability and claim it was a type of intelligence. So dancing became an intelligence. And this is why there are daft degrees in trivial activities that pretend to involve intelligence. Students expressed great offence – all part of clinical narcissism – if it was hinted that they were doing a pointless degree at a bogus university and were clearly victims of some marketing hype.

The theorists were right about the relationship between self-esteem and (academic) success but wrong about the direction of causality. Doing well is the cause, not the result, of high self-esteem. Working on self-esteem in the hope that it brings success simply feeds narcissism. And narcissism is a hungry and fragile plant.

Healthy self-regard comes from finding strengths, working on them and building a skill base. It all involves hard work, dedication and resolve. Ask Olympic athletes. And from that investment self-esteem flows.

So what happened to humility? Nearly all the world religions condemn arrogance and praise humility: the humble vs the proud; the David and Goliath story; the widow's mite; Jesus and the Pharisees. There are endless stories and parables that warn against the sins of arrogance: Pride is a deadly sin; selfishness and ignoring one's fellow man; vanity and the foolishness of chasing materialism over spiritualism.

Note the charm of the Amish and the strength of the Quakers. Amish adolescents can look sheltered, naïve and vulnerable. They seem to be throwbacks to another age. For Dawkinites, they have been brainwashed by a false creed and need Pol Pot style re-education camps. But which would you choose to teach or spend time with: a class of Amish, or Quakers, or a gang of inner-city, feral children who trumpet their rights?

Humility begets kindness. It is as attractive as hubris can be repulsive. But there are two other types of humility.

First, there is *British false humility* which always foxes the Americans. It is a game played less and less by academics, politicians and business people, but is still readily detectable. It can be spotted in how people talk about success. So you say, 'I was fortunate enough to be selected for Oxbridge/the Olympics/promotion to the board.' The idea is that you invoke luck to explain success. Not talent, hard work or family privilege.

The understatement continues when describing an occupation. The answer, 'I sell vacuum cleaners' or, 'I dabble in art' could mean that you are sitting next to Sir James Dyson or Charles Saatchi. The academic says, 'I really know very little about this topic but . . .' Or, 'Forgive my ignorance but . . .'

It is a trick, of course, but fulfils some important social rules. Arrogance, self-importance and being a show-off is a 'pretty poor show'; 'clearly not cricket'; 'both vulgar and stupid'. But believing in yourself, your cause, your ability, is absolutely fundamental. You have to be sufficiently strong to show weakness, sufficiently confident to be humble.

There are cases where a sort of bumbling humility is not thought so highly of by the British. This may be nicely illustrated by Churchill's famous comment on his great adversary, Clement Attlee.

'Mr Attlee is a humble man', said Churchill, 'but then he has a lot to be humble about.'

This is indeed very different from the second form of humility. This is the *dehabilitating and dangerous* kind. It is where the belief that putting yourself forward or first in any situation is morally wrong. The psychiatrists may call this 'dependent personality disorder'. These humble people are badly abused by their selfish colleagues.

Often this humility is driven by psychological problems around inadequacy. Religions reinforce this. Consider the 'Prayer of Humble Access', which goes, 'We are not worthy, so much as to gather up the crumbs under thy table', or the many prayers of penitence. Clearly, religions can go too far in encouraging the believers to feel worthless in the sight of the Almighty. To be wracked by original sin and to be forever guilty about everything.

But best try the humility of those non-sacramental groups like the Quakers or the Salvation Army. People who remind themselves of how fortunate they are and how many are less so, and who set about doing something about it.

PART VI

Life Beyond

We hear a lot about work–life balance – not a very useful term, suggesting that life is the opposite or antithesis of work. But life outside work naturally influences how you perform at work. If a member of your family is ill, many aspects of work seem trivial and unimportant.

Many people report that they get some of their best ideas when on holiday, or taking the dogs for a walk at the weekend. In short, things that happen outside work can have great implications for inside work. There are lessons to be learnt on the sports field as well as meeting those who have chosen to live abroad.

A. DOG YEARS

It was always fun to calculate the age of man's best friend in 'dog years'. Multiply the dog's age by seven and you get it. So, a six-year-old hound should be well into a mid-life crisis and a nine-year-old looking forward to a pension. We are now told that this is rather too crude and there is a rubric which is a little more sophisticated: you multiple by 10.5 for the first two years and then by four for the years thereafter. So a three-year-old mutt is 25 years old and a five-year-old is a frisky 33-year-old.

And for cat lovers there is a different formula according to some sources. So two human years equals 24 cat years and 10 human years are 60 cat years. A 16-human-year-old cat is 84 . . . and possibly soon for the great cattery in the sky. Presumably you can do the same with all animals.

Churchill once famously remarked, 'I am fond of pigs. Dogs look up to us. Cats look down on us. Pigs see us as equals.' Yet as few of us keep the latter as pets, there seems to be far less interest in the human vs porcine years of your friendly porker.

For those interested in these things the Web offers a number of options about your time left – a comfortable euphemism meaning how long before you die. A variety of actuarial-type calculators attempt to predict that date that no man knows . . . the date of their death. All you do is enter some crude statistics: date of birth, alcohol and nicotine consumption, body mass index, your outlook on life and the country where you live. Press the button and, horrifically, a day is specified . . . the day you will die. Worse, some tell you how many years, months, days, hours and seconds you have left. Sobering, to say the least.

But there is some good news! First, these things are very unreliable . . . try doing three websites on offer and you will find they make very different predictions. Second, what about all those miracle advances in medical science which will prolong life and happiness considerably. Science will extend your life, adding a decade at least. Third, what about great uncle Arthur, who drank like a fish, smoked like a chimney, lived on bread and lard and died (very happily) in his sleep aged 94.

There are those who really can't abide this morbid, quasi-epidemiological forecasting. But is that denial and a refusal to confront one's mortality?

Yet reflectiveness does sell. In the recently published book *The Top Five Regrets of the Dying*, palliative care nurse Bronnie Warea noted the common themes from the many people she saw die. The first was about the many unfulfiled dreams that they had and now could not fulfil. The second was that they had spent too much time at work and not enough with family and friends. Third, they had never fully expressed their feelings and had carried the burden of bitterness for too long. Next, it was that they had lost touch with too many of their friends, though Facebook, LinkedIn and the rest should help that particular problem. And finally, the realization that happiness is a choice they did not always make.

Life is not a dress-rehearsal. Get on with it. Tomorrow is the first day of the rest of your life. But could this be a useful topic for a business seminar?

In the business training world there are various techniques designed to promote a bit of temporal introspection. One is to write your obituary: summarize what you have achieved in 600 words. Another has taken root and it goes like this: It is based on days of the week. You have to assume that a day's worth of time is 12 years and that we were all born in the first second on a Monday. By the end of that day we are 12 years old, and by the end of Tuesday 24. So calculate what day of the week you are at. If you are 42 you are halfway through Thursday and if you are 59, it is very late on Friday. Sunday midnight is game over, unless you are lucky enough to have a bank holiday bonus.

The 12-year bracket allows for enough discretion as to one's real age, though one suspects there are bound to be a few porkies or economies with the truth.

So the course delegates calculate their day. The Friday people might like to meet in a group to discuss. All rather alarming to see how old these people look, compared to your own youthful appearance, of course. Or perhaps it is better to mix the groups and discuss the possible advantages of mixed-age groups. But how about making three lists? What you will do in the time remaining, for yourself and family, for your organization and for your community. This lifts the spirit a little because it focuses on what to do rather than to simply sit there and mutter about so little time left. It also requires you to look beyond yourself, to think of others.

And after this morbid session of philosophizing in the office, you can go home to depress the dog and commiserate with the cat.

B. DRIVE FOR MONEY

The statistic that many people, particularly economists, find difficult to swallow is called the Easterlin hypothesis. Note, hypothesis not law – it's quite simple and the central question is 'How much money do you need to be happy?' and the answer is (only) about £40K–50K per annum. After that you get no 'hedonic bang for your buck'. So why do so many people chase money so remorselessly and so relentlessly? And at what cost? Do they not believe the statistic? Do they believe not only that greed is good but that it buys health, happiness and hedonism?

What do people appear to be prepared to forfeit for the almighty dollar? What is worth the sacrifice? The answer is threefold, and what is particularly interesting are the paradoxes in the whole business.

Perhaps our most valuable asset, a finite resource, is time. The older we get the more we know that to be true. Time is irretrievable. We have our three score and ten. You can't take it with you. There are no pockets in a shroud.

And yet, to buy time in leisure one has to sacrifice it in busyness. Long days become long years. Holidays are shortened. Work is done on holiday. And it saps up one's energy, enthusiasm, life-force.

Who was it that said that life is a bank account that offers only withdrawals, no deposits? You can't deposit sleep or time. It's finite.

And yes, the fantasy is to make one's pile, retire early to a life of leisure. But the slog transforms people. They experience burnout. They can't be playful or creative anymore. Life is grim and life is earnest. Work is all-consuming. It means for some that they are never able to experience real recreative leisure again.

The second sacrifice is linked to the first: it's mental and physical health. Sure, you can buy private medicine, psychotherapy and spa treatments. Long hours, a rich diet, few exercise opportunities, work stresses take their toll. Top executives often experience a wide array of psychosomatic illnesses, from migraine to irritable bowel syndrome as a result of chronic stress.

Hardly an ideal situation, working oneself to death. To sacrifice health for money and then try to buy it back again. But there is a third cost, more subtle but perhaps even costlier than the two above. It is the forfeiting of one's integrity, reputation and kindness. You have to be tough, wily and even callous in business to succeed. You have to kick ass, butt your adversaries and duck and weave around tax laws.

Not all successful people compromise their principles, but on the way up only the most ruthless do well. Perhaps that is why so many seem to try to buy their way out of an inaugural purgatory by giving vast fortunes away later.

It's true that money can't buy love, happiness or health but it has two other real allures. The first is best known as 'f***-off' money. It's the ability to tell anybody, anywhere to go away. Money is freedom. You are no longer beholden to bosses, shareholders, parents, spouses.

Money is freedom – not only from want but from the capricious demands, whims and dictates of others. Many rich, successful people experienced first-hand or saw in their parents the powerlessness that poverty brings. Seeing parents constantly struggle to survive: to have to give up dignity and health to please others. This is a serious driver of wealth.

But the second major attraction of money is not the material things it can buy, but rather it's a way of keeping score. It's very simple, very objective, very clean.

It's not really how much one has absolutely, but relative to significant others: pompous, privileged, acquaintances at school or university who patronize you; siblings who seemed cleverer or taller or more handsome. Early colleagues who did well.

Money means success. It is the best metric of success. And therefore it boosts self-esteem and a sense of self-worth. Indeed, for some it is worth having just because it puts others' noses out of joint. Nothing like being envied, Money doesn't talk – it shouts, it swears, it says, 'Hah look at me!'

Most people struggle with Maslow's 4th level: that of self-esteem. But for many, money shows you have made it. You have triumphed over adversity and won the race. You have literally earned self-esteem.

To be in the *Times* 100 is a triumph. But the problem with competitive social comparisons is that they are never satisfied. Being in the top 100 is not the same as the top 10, is not the same as number one. Once you play the game, you are trapped. If money is your major source of self-esteem you will never be released from the treadmill. And money makes you less trusting. To what extent are people who are polite, amused by your jokes and very complimentary about your appearance simply sycophantic, fawning, money grabbers? Can you buy respect or friendship? Alas not.

Happiness can't be bought. To some extent it is a trait, a habitual positiveness, a way of gaining social support from others. Possessions count for little, experiences a great deal.

So why the manic, fanatical, addictive drive for money? Part of the culture. But the fairy tales also very clearly state that it's a false god and that those who chase it really only derive any happiness from giving it away. Remember £50K. That's enough.

C. HAPPINESS BRINGS WEALTH

Economists (or at least some of them because as we know they can never agree with each other) seem to have lost one faith and gained another. The old faith was that money brought happiness. The new one is that happiness brings money.

It has been axiomatic to the practitioners of the dismal science that the pursuit of money is worthwhile. And, by and large, there is a linear relationship: more money, more happy. But then things started to go wrong. About 40 years ago, using population data, it was demonstrated that money had a very limited effect . . . after a modest amount (£50,000 a year) you got no happiness bang for your buck. It is ironic that so many so wealthy people appear to be so miserable. No simple pattern.

Of course, there has always been the debate between the spiritualists and the materialists about the power of money to satisfy basic needs. And between libertarians and socialists on how to spend money for the long-term benefit of all.

Then the psychologists started piling into the debate. We heard about the terrible disease of 'affluenza' that very rich people caught and which made them extremely unhappy. Psychologists have always argued that money is never a very good motivator at work. It sure has powerful and profound demotivational properties if you 'get it wrong', but, if you 'get it right', it has little effect.

There are four points the psychologists make. The *first* relates to the idea that the effects of a pay rise very soon wear off as people adapt to their new conditions. Money can be a very effective motivator, but you need a great deal of it to stop adaptation effects. Too much for most organizations to bear.

Second, what leads to pay satisfaction is not so much absolute salary but comparative salary. If my salary goes up dramatically, yet so does that of my comparison group, there is no change in my behaviour. No matter what people are paid, if they believe, with or without evidence, that they are not *equitably and fairly* paid, they become demotivated. The smallest differential can have the greatest effect.

Third, money is not everything; in fact, it may be much less important than health or holidays, time with the family and job security. People are prepared to *trade off* other things for money once they have enough, or grow weary of the game which is not worth the candle. The young, the desperate, perhaps the greedy, are willing to do anything for money. But are they the people on your payroll or the people whom you want to employ?

Fourth, there is the eternal implication of tax and spend . . . all very well to increase pay, but if increased taxes eat heavily into it, there can be marginal benefit. Why earn when the government takes too much? If the government takes 50 per cent and more . . . hardly worth the effort.

There has been research on people who achieve sudden wealth through lottery wins or inheritance. It shows that while there is an obvious and explicable boost in well-being after the money is obtained, within a year or two people revert to their 'previous level' of happiness. Sudden wealth brings only a short-term increase in happiness, and for a significant few it actually makes things worse.

So, money does not bring happiness. But what if the opposite were true? To test this hypothesis you need to follow up a group of people for quite a long time and be able to measure accurately both their happiness and well-being and also how much money they are making. Longitudinal studies of representative populations is good science. One can study the epidemiology of wealth.

And this is precisely what two British economists did. They studied 90,000 young people for seven crucial years from ages 22 to 29. And what did they find? People with a sunnier disposition were more likely to get a degree, get hired and get promoted . . . all of which related to income.

So the half-full glass fills up, but the half-empty glass evaporates. But how does this work? What is the mechanism which explains this causal relationship? Consider the following:

■ Optimistic, positive, life-enhancing, happy people are nicer to be around, so they receive more attention and are more likely to be selected for everything compared to their pessimistic, negative, life-sapping, miserable peers. That is why they are hired and promoted: all that 'can do', 'will have a go', 'sure, it's a pleasure' that you get from the sunny worker.

■ Happy people have better moods, which means they make better decisions and feel able to rise to greater challenges. Bad moods or general moodiness can easily affect clear thinking and decision-making.

■ Happy people are mentally and physically fitter . . . they are less prone to anxiety, depression, moodiness and psychosomatic disorders. This means they don't go absent much and don't miss out on things. They pitch up and pitch in more often and with more enthusiasm.

■ Happy people have better relationships: they are more attractive and have more friends who can be useful for a whole range of activities. We all need social support at times, and happy people have greater access to it.

So, buy one of those books on how to be happy. It may be a seriously good investment.

D. MIND AND SOUL OF THE EXPAT

How resilient are people when posted abroad? How do people respond to culture shock? They are truly ubiquitous. More so than traffic wardens or *Big Issue* sellers. From Aden to Adelaide, Bangalore to Brisbane, Dubai to Durban, Tripoli to Toronto, one finds the (British) Expat. No, they are not always in a Panama hat and crushed linen suit; nor wearing socks with sandals; or even propping up the bar under palm trees rather earlier than is acceptable. But they are recognizable. And there are many of them.

Possibly resulting from the adventure of Empire or the roller coaster of the British economy since the War, in the 20th century the country experienced net emigration not immigration, a total of over 15 million people. But things are changing. The recession in Spain has seen the return of droves of tanned but impoverished Brits who hoped to see out their days on the sun-kissed Costas. Even the Peter Mayle Francophiles are rerunning from their bucolic idylls due to economic factors. The Expats are coming home.

Some small countries, such as Ireland and New Zealand, have experienced the pain and loss of the 'mass' migration of their young people for decades. So sad to see the departure of the brightest and the best to countries with better job opportunities. Not always the most successful of course – there are also the adventurous, the naïve and the hopeful.

There are often powerful, pull-and-push factors involved in emigration. Things you get away from – joblessness, political instability, over-regulated societies – and things you are attracted to, such as a different lifestyle, entrepreneurial opportunities and social tolerance. The weather features high in talk about migration of course.

The Expat is not the same as the sojourner. Many people work abroad for a set task and time period. Posted to supervise a new start up, teach technical skills to the locals, introduce processes and procedures that are in line with agreed international standards.

Some lead the good life in luxurious, safe compounds that are little more than ghettos. Spouses are happy with the army of servants, the education and health facilities just for them, and the sunshine. Some get used to being sequential sojourners: diplomats, mining experts, missionaries, engineers. They move on from site to site, repeating much the same exercise for decades.

There are plenty of pretty accurate (and funny) stereotypes of the (British) Expat. There are those who 'go troppo'. Perhaps through boredom, drink or some mental breakdown they seem to have a tenuous grip on reality, regressing in their dress, habits and lifestyle to something between Robinson Crusoe and the Maharajah of Jaipur. Others behave as if they never left home. So in the middle of a thriving Asian city you find a Surrey suburbia of houses and people frozen in the time period when they left their native country. Perfectly preserved in the past – ideal subject matter for a television documentary. But often more sad than amusing.

There are some easy but important tests of Expat adjustment. The first is to listen to the way they talk about their home country. Is it with anger or nostalgia? Do they spend a lot of effort denigrating it as it is now or how it was then?

Psychologists call this reaction-formation. It's a defence mechanism whereby the opposite emotion is expressed. The idea is that un- or subconsciously they really want to return home but can't say so. In fact, this psychic energy causes a powerful reaction which leads them to spend long periods of time knocking the country of their birth.

Some Expats are economic prisoners. They may be unable to return due to the decline in their wealth or the devaluation of their currency. Others face significant downward mobility because they are massively overpaid compared to what they might receive at home. So they have dissonance. And the best way to resolve that is to knock their home country.

Another issue for the Expat is cutting all ties with home, usually by selling a property. Ask them where they intend to 'fetch up' after retirement. Ask them where they own property. Ask them whether they have given up their nationality. Are they dual nationals with dual allegiances? And is that really possible?

Some Expats do travel in every sense of the word. They do believe the past is another country. They are present- and future-oriented as opposed to past-oriented. They can let the past go. They admit to being products of their past, if not victims of it.

Many business people have a spell of work abroad. For some it is a sojourn with a deadline. They don't have to deal with many of the issues faced by the Expat, migrant or refugee. Some enjoy multiple tours of duty, becoming peripatetic '*Wandervogel*' following the dictats of their organizations. There are pull-and-push factors that cause migration. In the deep sentimentalism of Irish and Scots music you hear how much they felt push (usually by economic forces), not pull by excitement or promises of riches. Migration is about letting go, moving on and reframing. Easier to do, of course, when you are young. Easier when you want to go. Easier when you adapt well.

E. REGRETS

Television documentaries about prisoners on death row can hold a particular fascination for many viewers. It is revealing to ask people what they would do if they had just one month to live. Some start with consulting lawyers and accountants. Sort out the inheritance stuff. Some would immediately take off on a world tour, sparing no joy or experience en route. Others would spend as much time as possible with old friends and close family.

Some would phone up MI6 and offer to attempt to assassinate anyone currently on their hit list. Some would turn to any therapy or therapist that offered them a cure or any extra time. And some would spend a lot of time tidying their drawers, sorting out their stuff so that those left behind wouldn't have to.

A recent book on the regrets of the dying drew appropriate attention from many groups. Somehow the imminent threat of death focuses the mind. In that sense funerals are more psychologically 'useful' than marriages as they encourage reflection, which can cause beneficial change.

Regrets seem much more about what people *did not do* as opposed to what they did. The first regret seems to be about inauthenticity and seizing the day. It is when you do not have options that you realize how many you had. Dreams, ambitions and hopes were not fulfiled because people were too busy, too distracted, too procrastinating to do what they really wanted. This is a 'life is not a dress rehearsal' warning – now may be your only real opportunity.

Some seem to imply that they were too inhibited by the powerful forces of family and religion, convention and circumstance to do what they felt was right for them. So too much passed them by. They never did see the Taj Mahal, go swimming with the dolphins, hire a Roller for the day.

Another regret is similar, except it relates to feelings: 'I wish I'd had the courage to express my feelings.' Presumably this refers to strong feelings – both positive and negative. It used to be thought that keeping in feelings, particularly anger, was related to cancer. The emotionally repressed, resentful, deeply frustrated and angry person was prone, it was said, to cancer. And those with anger management problems were prone to heart attack. Too much anger in or out and you were done for!

Certainly, there are heartrending stories of people – usually men – who felt unable or too inhibited to express their love for their children (usually sons) or friends. They go to their grave never having shown or spoken about the profound gratitude that they felt towards relatives, neighbours or teachers.

All that homophobia, stoicism and sangfroid stopped them saying what they deeply felt until it was too late. Indeed, people are encouraged by the positive psychologists to write gratitude letters and make calls expressing positive feelings to others, if they are genuinely held. Good for both parties.

And some regret never having told selfish, bullying bosses how much you and others despised them. Or nosy relatives, egocentric friends or demanding neighbours how much you resented them. It's called being assertive – not passive or passive-aggressive. It's about honest feedback. About being able to express the depth and complexity of one's feelings to others. Sad, indeed, to take them to the grave.

Next, there was the issue of keeping up with friends. Perhaps Facebook and Friends Reunited have ameliorated this problem. Maybe the Web helps us trace and stay in touch, even if only electronically. There is a skill in making friends, some effort in maintaining relationships. But there is also great reward. One can be sustained by friendship, supported in bad times, share triumphs. And, of course, friends carry your memory.

Friends can be sources of comfort and honesty. They can give without counting the cost. They can provide all-important social support when down and rejoice in your successes. Unhappy is the man who lays down his friends for his life.

Another regret is 'I wish I'd let myself be happier.' Ah, the existentialists were right then. Suffering is a choice. So is happiness? This regret is all about fear of change, comfort blankets, self-pretence. It is all about fun-aversion – not laughing loudly and openly with others at the sheer pomposity, stupidity and daftness of people. People regret not having been naughty and silly. They regret caring about what people think of them and not doing little, often childlike things that bring extreme pleasure that are constrained by inner and outer forces. So giggling, naughtiness and other signs of happiness are prevented.

But it is the next regret that is most interesting. Apparently *every* male patient said they wished they had not worked so hard. It took them away from their children's youth and partner's companionship. Odd in some ways. For some men work is a refuge from unhappy relationships and difficult families. It also presumes that friendships at work can never be as good, long-lasting or fulfilling as those in the home. Can't work be absorbing, fulfilling and a place when you can express your passion and vitality, and explore and exploit your real skills?

F. SPORTS ETHIC

Even the most talented, medal-winning Olympian athlete is likely to have a short career. Mainly for physical reasons, many are finished in their early 1930s, though some sports are a little more forgiving. Years and years of amazingly dedicated practice and you are left career-less and probably with some semi-serious injuries.

What is their fate? There are some attractive options: become a national coach, turn to media commentary, start your own brand. Becoming a PE teacher or working in a sports shop seems rather a come-down after all that effort and glory.

Some ex-sports stars have tumbled to a newish and very well-paid wheeze: *motivational speaking*. Go to the website of those who offer a range of celebrity speakers and you find among the politicians, academics and business people a long list of sports people. Some, perhaps many, you have never heard of; masters of a sport you are even less sure about.

But most business people will have heard a famous(ish) sports person speak at a conference. They may be round-the-world sailors, sprinters, boxers or rowers. It's a nice little earner if you are any good and get asked frequently. Many are, alas, not cut out for the role, which demands a certain flair and style that is not required on the field, court or pool.

The athlete's story can be very dull, often because, quite clearly, it is. It is all about spending years doing the same thing day after day for months on end, working towards an event that lasts less than 30 minutes, four years hence. And the audience is invited to try to work out, in their break-out rooms, how all this is remotely relevant for them at work. The better speakers do it for you. They have usually worked out that the work ethic and the sports ethic share a great deal.

Most of us have been inculcated with the idea that sport builds character. We know about 'the playing fields of Eton' and 'play up and play the game'. Of how the games master could inspire things the maths teacher could not. And of how the near-delinquent were turned around after discovering their talents at particular sports.

Some of the sportsmanship values seem particularly relevant today: adhering to the rules, accepting the official's decision (none of that rage-fuelled 'you can't be serious' talk). Outwardly upholding the regulations of the governing sport. It is about all those good things such as integrity, reliability, honesty. Being candid, sincere, forthright. Being utterly trustworthy. Having the courage to live by principles.

Rule number one: no cheating (i.e. drugs), no knifing opponents in word and deed. No put-downs, insults, ridiculing others. Being totally honest and respectful. Accepting personal accountability and understanding legal and moral obligations.

There are many other values that are part of the sports ethic which are music to the ears of many employers:

Competition: All understand that competition is good. It drives up standards/records and is the only way to produce the best in their area. It is about fair play and justice, but also about standing out as 'best in class'.

Universalism: Sport is open to all, irrespective of all those discriminatory 'isms': age, class, creed, sex. It does, of course, have a lot to do with shape. But the message is clear: you are judged entirely and exclusively on the quality of your performance. All that counts is sporting prowess. So, opponents have to be treated with courtesy, dignity and tolerance. Nepotism and favouritism are a no-no.

Diligence: Nothing is achieved or achievable at international standard without hard work, fortitude and perseverance. You can only succeed if you make personal sacrifices, take part in long, strenuous preparation and have stamina for the journey. You have to pursue excellence relentlessly.

Success: This is everything; coming second is not good enough. You play to win, to get the accolades and prizes that come with being first. This is the opposite of the 'all shall have prizes' philosophy. No, not everybody is creative, or intelligent, or gifted 'in their own special way'. Success is for the few who have the right mix of ability and effort.

Self-discipline: You have to lead a life of ascetic self-discipline and self-control. All your habits need to be healthy. It is about resisting temptation for long periods of time. Sacrificing many pleasures of the flesh for your goal.

Magnanimity: Learning to be gracious in defeat and able to admire openly those better than yourself. Hubris is a sin, humility a virtue. Though you might not believe it, you have to talk about how lucky you were, not how deserving.

There are some values of great importance that do not apply to all sports. Perhaps the most important is *teamwork*. This is about co-operation, trust and support. It is about being totally loyal to your colleagues and as concerned for their welfare as your own. It is about learning how to be neither dependent nor independent, but interdependent.

Shrewd observers and sceptics may notice that some of these values seem somewhat contradictory and contain ambitious sentiments that are little related to reality.

Yet the games went well have begun: all day, every day, the world's top athletes were the visible embodiment of these values, perhaps even more so in the Paralympics. All competitors, particularly the medal winners demonstrated the result of hard work and self-sacrifice and perhaps inspiring the population to try harder and achieve more. They are essentially motivational speakers for the nation.

You do not have to be interested in sport at all to admire the determination and sacrifice of successful athletes. They are the very essence of the concept of Resilience.

Printed and bound by CPI Group (UK) Ltd, Croydon, CR0 4YY